20 TEACHABLE VIRTUES

20
TEACHABLE
VIRTUES

Practical Ways to Pass on
Lessons of Virtue and Character
to Your Children

BARBARA C. UNELL
and JERRY L. WYCKOFF, Ph.D.

A *Perigee Book*

A Perigee Book
Published by The Berkley Publishing Group
200 Madison Avenue
New York, NY 10016

Book design by Irving Perkins Associates

Cover design by Karen Gover

Cover illustration by Linda Montgomery

First edition: August 1995

Published simultaneously in Canada.

Library of Congress Cataloging-in-Publication Data

Unell, Barbara C.
    20 teachable virtues : practical ways to pass on lessons of virtue and character to your children / Barbara C. Unell and Jerry L. Wyckoff.
        p.   cm.
    "A Perigee book."
    ISBN 0-399-51959-9 (pbk. : alk. paper)
    1. Moral education. 2. Virtues — Study and teaching.   I. Wyckoff, Jerry.   II. Title.   III. Title: Twenty teachable virtues.
LC268.U54   1995
370.11'4 — dc20   94-41671
                                                            CIP

Printed in the United States of America

10   9   8   7

This book is printed on acid-free paper.

May our children — Amy Elizabeth, Justin Alex, Christopher Britt, and Allison Leigh — understand that their ethical roots can be found here with us in this family book of character and virtue . . . even as their lives will surely lead them to adventures far away in body, but not in spirit, from each of their families. May these virtues always shine brightly within them, illuminating their paths wherever their dreams may lead, as they lit the way for so many generations before them.

Contents

ACKNOWLEDGMENTS

WE LOVED WRITING THIS book. We loved seeing the joy that these 20 teachable virtues create in those who practice them. In fact, we became hopeful, at times even giddy, about America's future generations as we envisioned families truly embracing, in everyday interactions, these behaviors that will lead them down so many time-worn, fragrant, virtue-filled growth paths together, just as families have done in countless generations gone by. We loved spending many, many hours ruminating about these good things — the best of what humans can offer each other. And finally, we simply loved the image of kindhearted adults truly "trying on the shoes" of their children, and vice versa, as they developed empathy behaviors in their families — the true core virtue that makes human life so valuable.

As we honed in on just what stories to tell and examples to use in 20 *Teachable Virtues*, we were repeatedly encouraged, cheered on by hundreds of caring colleagues, teachers, parents, friends, and neighbors who, like us, heard America's clarion call for a practical, easy-to-use book that focuses on what to "teach," instead of what to "moralize," to one's children concerning lessons of virtue.

Many wonderful pearls of wisdom were discovered as we shared the growth of this book with those near and dear to us. It was in the quiet models of our families that we both received our first brush with virtue, and were first inspired by their examples of a strong work ethic and moral principles upon which they worked and played. And it was in the offices of Kathleen Currence and Betty Lewis, the classrooms of Lynn Granger, Jackie Lenz, Teresa Hogan, and Robin Hodges, the cozy kitchen of Elaine Nelson, and miles of walks and talks with Cathy Alpert, SuEllen Fried, Margaret Martin, Adele Hall, Ellen Hamilton, Rita Blitt, Marcia Biel, Mary Ann Hale, Mary Shaw Branton, Page Reed, Daniel Brenner, and dozens of colleagues that much of this book took on a life of its own. Our thanks also to the children of Overland Trail Middle School, Tomahawk Ridge Elementary School, and Santa Fe Trail Elementary School for sharing their thoughts on 20 *Teachable Virtues* as quoted throughout this book.

Through our membership in the Character Education Partnership, we have been fortunate to know many people who also deserve a standing ovation for their uncompromising willingness to dig deep into their hearts and minds to teach these lessons of virtue to their students throughout America. A big hug to our agent, Susan Ann Protter, whose belief in this project and in the power of living a virtuous life kept this ship on course. Without the dedication and tenacity of the staff of *Twins Magazine*, Jean Cerne, Bob Hart, and Cindy Himmelberg, in particular, the dream of this book just might still be swirling around wildly inside our heads. Kudos also to the amazing Cathy Diggs, who so capably kept us afloat and sailing smoothly amidst the amazing volume of work generated over this virtuous passage.

We are deeply indebted to Robert Unell and Millie Wyckoff, who understand that this book simply *had* to be born and gave us their empathy, patience, and care during its creation. To the distinguished Thomas Lickona, we owe our heartfelt gratitude for striking a match that truly ignited the flame of character education that burned so much brighter within us after reading his wonderful book *Educating for Character*.

And most especially . . . our thanks to our editor, John Duff, for believing. And for the gifts of mutual respect and friendship that have grown from this magical book.

"I always prefer to believe the best of everybody — it saves so much trouble." — RUDYARD KIPLING

PREFACE

*"Always do right. This will gratify some people,
and astonish the rest."* — MARK TWAIN

> **vir·tue** *n.* **1.** moral excellence; goodness; righteousness **2.**
> conformity in life and conduct to moral and ethical princi-
> ples **3.** a particular moral excellence **4.** a good or admirable
> quality as of a person, thing, etc. **5.** inherent power to produce
> effects; potency

THE FIRST AND MOST important teacher of virtues and
character an infant can have is a caring adult. Through the
guidance of such a caregiver, each child can learn what it
feels like to trust that someone will always be there to give
unconditional love and provide for his or her basic needs.
This experience of receiving unconditional love is the first
lesson upon which all other lessons of virtues and character
are built. This gift of unconditional love is given freely to this
child, simply because he or she is a precious human being. It
is given without reservation, without expectation of return,
and with no strings attached, regardless of the child's behavior.

In the context of this love, babies begin to learn what is
"right" and "wrong" through interacting with their environment and discovering that this significant adult places limits
on what they are and are not allowed to do. Thus begins the

process of an infant becoming a person who can live in a civilized world.

Learning these lessons about "right" and "wrong" may come easily to some children and with more difficulty to others, depending on how well they are able to handle not getting their wants satisfied immediately and how readily they conform to the greater good of the social group as a way of gaining the approval of the caring adults around them. This fact is crucial for families to realize because this molding of the good moral, virtuous character of children depends on two major variables: the distinctive makeup of the "clay" (individual assertiveness/passivity, extroverted/introverted, gloomy/cheerful, quiet/loud, shy/outgoing, and in some views, male/female) and the learned skills of the parent or other caregiver "sculptors" who are molding the clay that can vary within the same family and even within the same day.

Nevertheless, to learn to live in society, all children must learn to balance their personal wants against the needs of the social group (family, neighborhood, school, society). Today we see far too few examples of this kind of balance as people put their own wants and needs above all others — all of the time. With this book, you, the sculptors, can teach your children, the clay, the virtues necessary to create that kind of balance and make a meaningful contribution to family and society while becoming the kind of responsible, caring, likable human beings you both want them to become.

"If you are a parent, recognize that it is the most important calling and rewarding challenge you have. What you do every day, what you say and how you act, will do more to shape the future of America than any other factor." — MARION WRIGHT EDELMAN

INTRODUCTION

"If I am not for myself, who is for me? And if I am only for myself, what am I? If not now, when?"
— HILLEL

IDEALS. HOPES. DREAMS. INNOCENCE. When images of the whole world's cruelest realities — war, abuse, violence of all kinds — are instantly accessible at the touch of a button or the flip of a page, it's hard to remain idealistic, hopeful, positive, imaginative. When nothing is left to the imagination, it's hard to become impressed or in awe of new, fresh, untouched territory. When the dark side of human nature — the stormy, troubled side — is the pervasive picture of former heroes and heroines of politics, entertainment, and sports, it's hard to feel supportive and trustful of our fellow human beings.

So no wonder it's difficult these days for children to grow up amidst the storms in our turbulent society. And no wonder that so many of us wring our hands and worry in the stillness of the night, or cluck and squawk in the fast-paced clatter around the water coolers of our respective offices: "What a mess these kids are growing up in!" we lament. And yet, solutions that each of us can implement to help the storms become sunny skies don't seem, at first glance, to be able to whisk away the clouds.

"Why even try?" some say. The problems seem so big, the people in charge so far away, so powerful, so wealthy, so far removed from our living rooms, our offices, our schools.

Feelings of helplessness plague us as we see our younger children — even toddlers — being taught the very lessons that we *don't* want them to learn from their peers, the media, school violence, fallen heroes. Why even try?

But we know from our daily living that the only thing to do when there's a mess is to clean it up: learn to keep things neater, more organized every day, and feel satisfied when the hard work of cleanup is done. And that, our friends, is what this book is all about — everyday cleaning-up of the way we treat ourselves, our families, our neighbors, each other. And for this job, it is precisely you and I who are in charge.

This book is testimony to a celebration of the fact that we are each in charge of preventing and/or cleaning up the mess of our character-starved, immorally littered world. This climate of virtues in which we all want children to grow can be created by looking into our hearts, souls, and minds and teaching the lessons that we know need to be taught — the very lessons you are holding in your hand.

Think of this book as your personal toolbox to clean up your individual environments, an individual commitment you are making to stop the pollution of our children's lives with models of irresponsibility and dishonesty. It's a wake-up call to say "Enough is enough!"

"I can do this!" I tell my friends at the water cooler and tell myself in the still of the night. "I am committed to my children to help them learn the time-tested, generations-old, universally agreed-upon virtues of good character outlined in this book. I know that I want to raise children who have these virtues! I just need to know how to do it!" I say.

We promise that learning how to teach the lessons in this book to your children will be nothing short of an awesome experience for you: You, as well as your children, will learn to be more compassionate, less fearful, and more respectful of yourself and more positive about the future of all families as you learn the behaviors of 20 *Teachable Virtues* together as a family.

That these twenty virtues have always been seen as the basic tenets upon which a civil, moral, and just society has operated is undeniable. That they can slip out of our daily, prioritized rules of living, as families become busier and more mobile, is also undeniable. The good news is that we can incorporate these virtues into the nourishment that we provide our children every day at a lower price than neglecting to do so. When we continue to pass on these lessons to the next generation, just as our grandparents passed them on to our parents and our parents did to us, we will be giving a gift so precious and priceless that it will continue to increase in value beyond our lifetimes . . . for it will be the foundation of family life for generations to come.

The responsibility to teach these twenty virtues rests squarely in our hands. No other institution but the family can pass the baton of these virtues as meaningfully and comfortably as the family. It is within these individual patchwork quilts of common history, shared genetics, and loving and familiar environments that the universal foundation of strong human character — empathy, responsibility, caring, and trust — with which these virtues are woven truly lies. As imperceptible as a fallen eyelash, our models of virtue fall on bone dry, young sponges each day — sponges just ready and waiting to breathlessly absorb these essential life lessons.

"To educate a person in mind and not in morals is to educate a menace to society." — THEODORE ROOSEVELT

HOW CHILDREN LEARN

Currently, talk about virtue, values, morals, and character has emerged in the forefront of movement for social change. However, it is important to understand that these traits must be taught rather than talked. For our society to heal itself and to develop into an enduring culture with a core of virtue, children must be taught the behaviors of virtue. With the book you are holding as your guide, we are proud to make this journey of learning together.

Because children are fairly concrete in their view of the world, it is difficult to teach them concepts that are too abstract. Each of these twenty virtues is an abstract set of concepts that may be difficult for some children to understand. Moreover, even if they can define the virtue, they may not have the skills available to be able to use it. That is why we broke each virtue down into behaviors that can be observed: so that children can learn how to do what is being asked of them in order for them to become children of strong character. Parents should not worry about the attitudes of children, because attitudes are hypothetical constructs that are inferred from behavior. Behavior change precedes attitude change, so if attitude change is needed, we first must change behavior by teaching new, more appropriate behavior.

There are proven ways children learn behaviors that can be used to teach virtues to them. To become good teachers of behavior, or any lesson, parents must follow these basic steps:

1. Set goals for the children to achieve.
2. Define the behaviors that will be needed to reach the goals.

3. Model the behaviors so the children will have a mental picture of what they are.
4. Encourage the children's practice of the behaviors.
5. Reinforce the practice through the use of praise and privileges.
6. Observe the children in order to decide whether the behaviors have been learned.

"There's only one corner of the universe you can be certain of improving, and that's your own self."
—ALDOUS HUXLEY

HOW TO FIT VIRTUES INTO FAMILY LIFE

As a society, we have lost the art of reflection, that ability to think deeply and meaningfully about issues. Instead, through media glitz and glitter, hype and pizzazz, we have learned only to feel what others are feeling as we vicariously experience what others are experiencing right before our eyes. By only reacting emotionally, we are giving our tacit approval to what we are witnessing without evaluating whether it is right or wrong, moral or immoral, ethical or nonethical, whether or not it meets our own personal rules of living. We have replaced thought with emotion.

However, essential to the teaching of virtues is the development of this most important ability to reflect on life's experiences. Learning from experiences depends on the ability to reflect on those experiences and to develop new, more appropriate ways of behaving. With our responses to experiences limited to emotion, we end up with the image of virtue without having virtues as a part of our way of life.

Teaching these twenty virtues to your children begins with the awareness that they are the basis of your own definition of good character. Notice how you react when someone gives you back more change than you were due at the grocery store. What do you say when someone calls and wants to talk when you're in the middle of dinner or other personal activities? How do you respond when your son arrives ten minutes later than the time when you were supposed to pick him up?

Establishing your own personal living standards and living by those standards involves no magic, only the setting of priorities and the active choosing of moral and ethical ways of behaving over the self-centered, what's-in-it-for-me, win-at-all-costs approach to life that has become the vogue. Virtues are not taught by force-feeding. In fact, just the opposite is true. The teaching of virtues is undertaken in the everyday interactions with children: during the jaunt to the shopping center, standing in line at the fast-food restaurant, traveling full tilt to ball practice.

So if it's so easy to do, this practicing of virtues, why don't more of us do it? Because it takes considerable effort — hard work — to discipline ourselves to do so. At times it may seem easier to yell and scream, to clean up children's rooms ourselves instead of going through the hassle of teaching children to do so, to be critical of others, and to find someone to blame for the problems that, at first blush, we can't seem to solve. This is particularly true if we were parented by folks who modeled these behaviors.

It is a proven fact that the lessons of virtue in this book are best learned from those who practice what they teach. Changing your behavior from what you learned about parenting as a child to what you want to pass on to your children can be accomplished if you open your mind and heart to these lessons that have been passed on for generations but may, in fact, be new to you. By putting new "deposits" in your "teaching bank" through using this book, you are, in fact, making that first investment. The joy, love, and hope that will grow from this investment is guaranteed safe by the FDIC (the Family Deposits in Caring), whose laws of doing business are as follows:

The FDIC

1. Be there as a positive role model when your children truly need you — let your children know they can trust you to do so.
2. Develop a consistent, fair discipline plan.
3. Use unconditional love, kindness, and caring in enforcing discipline.
4. Avoid power struggles with your children.
5. Model the virtues being taught.
6. Decide on family priorities.

"He who conquers others is strong: He who conquers himself is mighty." — LAO-TZU

HOW TO USE THIS BOOK

THIS BOOK FOLLOWS an easy-to-read format that is similar to the format of our books *Discipline Without Shouting or Spanking* and *How to Discipline Your Six-to-Twelve-Year-Old Without Losing Your Mind.*

In each chapter you will find ways to take simple, everyday experiences and make them special and satisfying "Teachable Moments" full of lessons of virtue. As a means to this end, we often discourage the use of extrinsic reinforcement, such as material rewards, for appropriate behavior. However, we have encouraged the use of coveted activities and privileges as motivators for appropriate behavior. The latter recommendation is called "Grandma's Rule." This rule is beneficial because it helps children make their responsibilities, however they are defined as they grow, a higher priority than their "play." In contrast, extrinsic, material reinforcement teaches this undesirable lesson: Feeling proud of the effort one has made is not enough reason, in and of itself, to do something. This "what's in it for me?" attitude develops from children's expectation that they must get money, stickers, candy, and the like before they agree to do something.

To help you use the "Teaching Tool" of Grandma's Rule, and so many others, in your own family, we have created a "sample family" in each chapter and have demonstrated how this family taught their children a particular lesson and what pitfalls they avoided in the course of doing so. The pitfalls—termed "Warnings"—are included in each chapter, to demonstrate that what might seem, at first glance, to be a positive way to teach a virtue can instead result in the learning of a lesson you *don't* want taught!

Each fictitious family has children of certain ages, but regardless of age, the suggested Teaching Tools that follow are appropriate for your family, because they each take advantage of the research concerning how children best learn a lesson and how that lesson can best be taught. For simplicity of reading, we have used the pronoun "he" when referring to a child of either sex.

The book begins with the virtue empathy, the core virtue around which all others in this book are built. Without the ability to behave with empathy—to put oneself in another person's shoes—the motivation for caring, honesty, trust, tolerance, and all the other virtues is lost to us. Therefore, you will find lessons in empathy as an ingredient in every chapter in this book.

"I celebrate myself and sing myself,
And what I assume you shall assume,
For every atom belonging to me as good belongs
to you." —WALT WHITMAN

EMPATHY

*"It is only with the heart that one can see rightly;
what is essential is invisible to the eye."*
—ANTOINE DE SAINT-EXUPÉRY

> em·pa·thy *n.* **1.** the imaginative projection of a subjective state into an object so that the object appears to be infused with it **2.** the capacity for participating in another's feelings or ideas

- "Mom! Are you all right? That must have hurt."

- "Mommy, that's heavy. Don't hurt yourself."

- "Hey, Mom, take it easy! Here, let me help you."

AHH . . . THE SWEET SOUNDS of empathy — endearing music to our ears. Can we really *teach* our children to say these things because they actually understand that another's welfare is important? Yes! This modified Golden Rule that many of our parents taught us is alive and well — and waiting to be taught to our children.

Why must you teach your children to "do unto others as you would have them do unto you"? Our answer: They need to learn behaviors that show empathy in order to help them live in peace with their neighbors, get along with their coworkers on the job, and enjoy relationships with friends and family. In fact, empathy is the rock-solid foundation for almost every brick used in building solid citizens of today and tomorrow. Empathy is the cement that holds together the secret formula for constructing caring and compassionate human beings, and it is as essential for our survival as air and water.

WHAT DO WE MEAN BY EMPATHY?

○ Empathy involves the ability to understand and to assume the role of another person.

○ In order to feel empathy, a child must be able to recognize and understand the emotions of others, and then be able to share those emotions.

○ By three years of age, most children have developed an awareness of themselves, and through that self-awareness, they become capable of feeling and showing empathy. But without teaching and reinforcing empathy, this ability will not be retained or used.

○ Generally by the time they are three years old, children show empathy when someone else is hurt, an experience the child has had by then and through which he can recall his own emotions.

○ Children who have a secure attachment to at least one adult have greater ability to feel empathy for others than those children who lack such a secure attachment.

"I learned so much about empathy from my mother and a little from my teachers. Empathy is so important. To be understanding of one's feelings is a key to friendship, my mom always said." —CARA BETH

Meet the Jones Family

Chris Jones, aged nine, and his eight-year-old sister, Allison, were experts in getting on each other's nerves. In fact, they were driving each other crazy! At times, Chris seemed merciless in his teasing of his sister, particularly after what seemed to be a long day. Their parents, Sam and Nancy, not only felt sorry for Allison but also realized that Chris was not a "mean child." The trouble in the Jones family stemmed from the fact that neither of their children had developed a set of behaviors that were empathic. They didn't know how to show they could relate to each other's frustrations.

Teaching Tools

Define empathy by example. Set a good example of ways that two people use caring when interacting with each other, so that each of your children will know what you are talking about when you use the word "empathy."

WARNING: AVOID DOING THE SAME THING TO THE CHILD THAT WAS DONE TO THE VICTIM.

Don't say. "Since you bit your sister, I'm going to bite you to let you know how it hurts." When young children hit or bite, it is tempting to do the same to them in order for them to experience the pain. When older children call names or hit each other, it is tempting to call them the same vicious names or to hit them in the same way. The old adage about sticks and stones but not words hurting you is fallacious. Words can cause pain, not only momentarily but also as scars that can last a lifetime inside your heart and mind. Unfortunately, children who experience punishment in kind only increase their anger and aggressiveness, lose respect for the adult who administers it, and reduce their ability to feel empathy.

Teachable Moment

"Wasn't it nice that your dad helped me clean up after dinner? He knew I was tired and could appreciate the help," Nancy Jones remarked casually to her children, hoping they would think of ways that they, too, could be nice to each other.

Later that day, Sam also took the opportunity to point out empathic behavior. "Your mom doesn't like to ask me to fix something for her when I first get home. She understands that I may have had a tough day and doesn't want to add to my stress."

Throughout the week, Sam and Nancy took every opportunity they could to call attention to the respect that they showed each other. "Thank you for bringing me the blanket," Nancy said to Sam, for example. "You understood that I was cold and could really use it."

Making these comments to their children helped Chris and Allison relate to real-life examples of the behavior that their parents wanted them to learn.

Develop a positive discipline plan. Parents who consider discipline a teaching process teach their children appropriate behavior by using consistent, fair, and nonviolent reprimands for inappropriate behavior. This technique uses empathy, understanding, and caring as the basis for its success even in the face of their children's cruel and unusual forms of punishment that they dish out to their friends and family.

WARNING: AVOID OVERREACTING.

When your children's nasty put-downs rear their ugly heads, don't say, "How dare you say things like that to your sister! Because you are being so mean to her, you are grounded for a month." Becoming overly upset, as in this example, suggests a loss of affection and support, and makes a child more angry and aggressive. This kind of overreaction not only fails to teach anything about empathy but also sets up a defiant reaction which can cause a child to reject the goal of empathy.

Teachable Moment

"I'm sorry you have chosen to fight rather than to get along with each other," Nancy said to Chris and Allison, who had been at each other's throats all morning.

"But she started it . . ." Chris began, only to be cut off by Nancy, who said, "It doesn't matter who started it. Your job is to get along. Now, let me tell you what your choices are: You may either choose to get along with each other and try to work things out between you. That way, maybe you will both feel good about caring about each other, as well as be free to do what you like to do today. Or you may choose not to cooperate with each other and work for me. You need to choose how you want to spend the day."

This proposal painted Chris and Allison a clear picture of which choice would be more rewarding, particularly when Nancy and Sam would compliment their children on how well they were getting along as the afternoon progressed. "Thank you so much for getting along with each other," Nancy said as she watched them playing a video game together. "Good getting along," Sam told them as they played independently in the same room. Getting positive attention from those whose opinion they most value helped reinforce Chris and Allison's decision to play together in harmony.

By having to bear the consequences of their actions when they did fight, the children learned that the benefits of listening to each other, cooperating, and understanding each other far outweighed all the costs of behaving selfishly.

Use I-statements. I-statements are those that tell "you" how "I" feel. When you use I-statements, you can avoid accusing and blaming someone and begin to express your feelings honestly. In order to use I-statements effectively, first decide what you want your position to be. Next, state the position while avoiding saying "you did . . . ," which accuses another of wrongdoing. When your children show a lack of empathy, use I-statements as a way of presenting the problem. Doing so will help you clear the air during confrontations without causing hurt feelings and defensive reactions.

WARNING: AVOID TAKING SIDES IN DISPUTES.

DON'T SAY: "I think you, Chris, were the one starting the fight. Go to your room now, Chris!" When children, especially siblings, are in conflict, taking sides or trying to get to the bottom of the problem may actually increase rivalry. Instead, help both children understand their contribution to the conflict, the feelings each has about the conflict, and how to go about problem-solving that will resolve this dispute as well as future conflicts.

Say, "What's the problem? What can you do about it when this happens? What would you expect would happen if you did that? Let's try the solution you have picked to see how it will work out."

Teachable Moment

"I feel bad about the fighting that is going on between the two of you. When I hear the squabbling, I become concerned about your not caring for each other," Sam shared. By using I-statements, Sam was pointing out the impact the children were having on him, an important step in teaching empathy.

Nancy also used I-statements to show her children how she felt about their behavior. "I felt that no one cared about the condition of our home when I saw the mess that was left in the kitchen," she said. "I expected too much, I guess."

The more the Jones children understood that their behavior had an impact on their parents, the more chances they had to put themselves in their parents' positions. By doing so, they also realized that upsetting their parents made them (the children) upset, both of which they wanted to avoid.

Teach children to be aware of the impact of their behavior. Talk! Talk! Talk! When your children cross the line into "forbidden behavior," don't guess about whether or not they are aware of their insensitive language or actions. State the problem, the consequences, and then drop it. Your goal is to help your children understand the implications of their behavior while it is fresh in their minds.

WARNING: AVOID THE USE OF PHYSICAL PUNISHMENT.

Don't say: "What you said is so mean, I should slap your face so you'll know how your sister feels." Spanking or hitting children, or even threatening to, is painful and unproductive for many reasons, including the fact that it reduces children's desire to want to follow the violent authority's rules. In addition, used frequently and erratically, physical punishment results in high levels of aggression and hostility. Aggressive children who are punished will persist in, and even increase, their inappropriate behavior and become even more unresponsive to social disapproval. In short, physical punishment only induces anger and the desire for revenge.

Teachable Moment

"Look at what you've done! You've hurt Allison's feelings by what you said. I hope you wouldn't really want to do that," Nancy said to Chris after one of his more scathing remarks. Though she knew that what she said might lay a guilt trip on Chris, that was just the point. Nancy understood that guilt can help overcome the natural selfishness of young children, replacing it with a sense of empathy and desire to help the victim.

Creating a sense of guilt is different from shaming and character assassination, however, because it focuses on the problem behavior and not on the person. When "That was an inappropriate thing to say to your sister" is said as a reprimand, it points out to Chris the error in his behavior without telling him that he was a bad person. In this case, Nancy presented the goal of not hurting Allison, or anyone else, as an understood "given" which she had confidence that her child would meet, if he only knew the effect of his behavior. They pointed it out as a piece of information, not as an insult.

Use role-playing as a way of teaching empathy. Remember the old saying "I'd walk a mile in his shoes"? Try putting your children in each other's shoes — literally, if that's possible. Then ask them to think about the feelings and emotions of their sisters, brothers, Mom, or Dad. When children even mentally experience the pain, fears, joys, and challenges that others experience, they are more likely to feel empathy toward them. When name-calling occurs, immediately go into theater mode, helping the villain become the victim for a few minutes.

Teachable Moment

After hearing Chris once again put his sister down, Sam said, "Because you like to call Allison names, it would be good for you to experience how she feels. I want you to pretend for a minute that you are Allison and you have been called the same names that you called her. Now, how would you feel?"

After a few moments of reflection, Chris answered, "I don't think I'd like it much."

By allowing Chris to "experience" the name-calling thrust upon his victim, he was able to feel what the target of his attack felt during his "bombing" of her, an experience that motivated him to choose to be caring, not unkind, to his sibling, just as he would want her to be to him.

"I think it's important to be understanding of others and to know how they feel when they're sad." — NICHOLE

Set behavior boundaries. Ever hear of giving children a "fair warning"? Telling children exactly what behavior you expect of them is "fair," because everyone then has an equal chance to meet these expectations. Fair warnings also help children feel secure, because they know the rules. A simple rule of thumb to follow: Children who understand the rules are less likely to make mistakes in following them.

Teachable Moment

One day when Chris had a friend over to play, Nancy overheard the boys verbally attacking Allison.

"Calling people names is inappropriate and will not be tolerated in this house," she told them. "I don't want you to do that regardless of whether or not you think anyone deserves it. If you have a problem with someone, we can help you work it out. When you choose to call someone names, you will be required to make up for that wasted time by working at a productive job assigned to you. So you need to decide whether you want to be free to do what you want or spend your valuable time working at things I want."

Setting consequences for rule violations ahead of time lets children predict what will happen if they break a rule. However, it is not always possible to know when a rule may be needed. Telling children what will happen, even after the fact, allows them to make choices about their behavior the next time they are tempted to avoid showing empathy.

Mediate television viewing time and other social influences on children. You can take your children's caring temperature by asking their personal reactions to things they see or hear while watching television programs together. From their answers, you can decide how much they understand and are affected by the behavior they witness.

Teachable Moment

While watching one program that both of their children agreed was cool, Nancy chose to ask these reflective questions (during commercials, of course), because they allowed her children to think about the impact of their behavior on other people and aided in their developing empathy:

"How do you feel when you hear people putting others down? What do you think about what happened in the show? What do you think your friends would feel about that? Can you imagine how behavior like that would be accepted at school, or on the street, if your parents or teachers acted like that? What do you think that behavior would do to the feelings of others?"

After the program was over, she added, "I really feel sorry for the other person when I see him being made fun of on programs. Nobody in my office talks to other people the way I hear them talk on TV. They'd probably be fired. I just think it's rude."

In the discussion that followed, both Chris and Allison demonstrated their understanding of how others feel by relating situations from school in which they had witnessed classmates being victimized by other classmates. Nancy was pleased that they understood the impact TV viewing was apparently having on some of their classmates, and could see the wheels turning inside their heads as they were amazed at the similarity of the put-downs on TV and those in their real world.

Mediate play activities. Everyone wants to be socially successful. But when your children play unsupervised, you cannot take advantage of any opportunities for teaching them the behaviors that lead to empathy. So try to stay close to your younger children's play activity in order to intervene when necessary to reinforce your family's rules. By doing so, you can help the positive aspects of peer activities remain in play while the negatives fade out of bounds.

Teachable Moment

When Nancy saw that her children were getting along well with other children or with each other, she said, "You both are getting along so nicely. Don't you feel good when you can be together without fighting?"

When her children weren't getting along, Nancy tried to mediate by problem-solving. "What's the problem? What choices do you have when a problem like this happens?" she would ask.

When choices were posed by her children, she said, "If you used that choice, what good things could you expect to happen? What bad things might happen? Would someone's feelings be hurt? Now, when you think about the good and bad things that might happen if you use a particular choice, do you want to try it to see if it works?"

This sort of problem-solving not only teaches conflict resolution but also teaches self-reliance and confidence in interacting with others, because children will know how to make getting along with others a priority.

Give positive attention for good behavior. When children are given positive attention (hugs, pats on the back, praise, etc.) for good behavior, they are more likely to repeat that behavior. Children thrive on positive attention, because it helps them feel secure and loved by those who they believe are most important to them.

WARNING: AVOID SHAMING YOUR CHILD.

DON'T SAY: "What you said to Allison was awful! You should be ashamed of yourself! You are such a mean, vicious person! It's a wonder anyone wants to be with you and be your friend." Inducing guilt, as in the example cited earlier in role-playing, can be helpful in motivating children to understand how others feel. However, you help children feel ashamed by saying, "Aren't you ashamed of yourself!" or "Shame on you," which decreases your child's ability to feel empathy. Such attacks on your child's character will only alienate him and reduce his ability to identify with a loving adult.

Teachable Moment

The moment to capture without waiting for a reply is this moment of truth: Sam and Nancy made the most of their children's *good* behavior by praising the jobs well done and offering time and attention as rewards.

"You did such a nice job vacuuming your room, Chris," Sam remarked after Chris had done this job as the consequence of calling his sister an unkind name. "You must feel proud of yourself for the effort you put into it."

Describing a behavior while giving it praise sets a goal for children to achieve in the future. Praise works best when it is specific to behavior (*"Nice getting along!"*) and is least effective when it describes the child (*"Good boy!"*) or does not specifically describe a behavior (*"Good job!"*).

Give reminders about the rules. Remember the game "Simon Says"? When you do what the leader and Simon say, you're still in the game. But if you do something that the leader says but Simon doesn't say, you're out. The same theory applies here: Before leaving children alone, even for a few minutes while you cook dinner in the next room, tell them what the rules are — what Simon says; that reinforces the virtues you want to establish in their character.

Teachable Moment

Sam and Nancy showed their confidence colors by expecting kind behaviors from their children and were consistent in enforcing the rule that play activities need to include cooperation. When disagreements occurred, they said, "Remember, you need to get along, share toys, and let me know if there is a problem you can't seem to work out. I'm sure you'll treat each other nicely while you play."

"Only when the sense of the pain of others begins — does man begin." — YEVGENY YEVTUSHENKO

2
_____

HELPFULNESS

"It is one of the most beautiful compensations of life that no man can sincerely try to help another without helping himself." —RALPH WALDO EMERSON

> **help** *vb.* **1.** to contribute strength or means to; render assistance to; cooperate effectively with; aid; assist **2.** to give aid; be of service or advantage

- "Here, let me help you with that! I'll get the door."
- "Mommy, I helped!"
- "It looks like you need some help."
- "I'll put my laundry on the stairs and take it up to my room later."

"HELP! I NEED SOMEBODY!" wailed the Beatles in one of their popular songs of the 1960s. "Help!" is a battle cry that, when shrieked in any language, signals the important roles people play in rescuing each other from danger and pain. With helpful behavior comes a satisfied feeling of doing something that can improve someone's life. Because doing is its own reward, when children learn to help others unselfishly they experience the good feelings that result from focusing on what others need, instead of *only* on what *they* want. Moreover, they learn the ability to put themselves in another person's position to see how others view the world. Only then can children learn how to live cooperatively together in harmony. The timeless children's classic *The Little Engine That Could* carries this theme as its soul — when someone offers to help, everything seems possible.

WHAT DO WE MEAN BY BEING HELPFUL?

○ Being helpful means giving without asking for anything in return.
○ In order to understand the need to be helpful, a child must learn to have empathy — the ability to put himself in another person's role.
○ To be helpful, a child must care about the person he is helping. The desire to be helpful comes from the desire to please.
○ Helpful people transcend their own needs and think of the needs of others, thereby acting from a base of caring and cooperation.
○ Being helpful truly means a child understands that the needs of others are to be considered as well as his own.

"My teachers tell me that being helpful is very impor-tant, like being nice to new kids or helping younger kids find their way to their next class." — JOYCE

MEET THE SHAFFER FAMILY

Six-year-old Amy and her eight-year-old brother, Arnold, seemed to think only about themselves and acted as if they cared little about what other family members needed. They could walk past their stacked laundry for days without seeming to notice that it needed to be taken to their rooms. Their parents, Lynn and Elaine, could break their backs carrying groceries, but their children wouldn't even hold the door open for them. They were so caught up in their own lives that they often didn't realize that there were others in the world.

TEACHING TOOLS

Assign children regular chores. Children who are given assigned chores begin to appreciate the effort needed to take care of their home, their belongings, their family's "space," as well as themselves. Only then can they learn about the need to be helpful to others. Three kinds of chores need to be done in a family: self-help chores that keep a child clean and presentable, family chores that maintain order and peaceful living in the family, and difficult "extra jobs" around the house which are done to earn money.

WARNING: AVOID PUNISHING WHEN CHORES ARE NEGLECTED.

Punishment leads to anger and resentment and reduces the desire to be helpful. Rather than punish children, let the natural consequences of not getting to do some fun activities do the teaching.

Teachable Moment

To begin their education in helpfulness, the Shaffers gave each of their children a list of age-appropriate chores that they needed to do each day to take care of themselves . . . simple stuff, such as putting their clothes in the hamper, making their beds, hanging up their towels after bathing, and straightening their rooms. After this list was presented, the tough job was being firm about enforcing the rule. Naturally, the children resisted doing their newly assigned chores.

"Let me tell you the deal here. When your chores are finished, you may do what you want to," Elaine said. This rule was the basis of the contract that Amy and Arnold's parents made with their children.

In the morning, for example, Amy didn't have to be reminded to make her bed. She knew that this chore had to be finished before she could play with her friends.

"I learned a lot about being helpful. That is one of my mom's top priorities. She taught me to do things without being asked to do them." —CARA BETH

Use a checklist to remind children about their chores. There are two ways to manage people: They can be directed to do things as the need arises, or they can be given objectives and can decide when and how to do what is needed. Giving children a checklist (illustrations can be used for pre-readers) allows them to work on their own for a whole day without having to be reminded or directed in what needs to be done.

WARNING: AVOID NAGGING CHILDREN ABOUT THEIR ASSIGNED CHORES.

Children don't learn to be independent and to take care of themselves when they are nagged; they learn only to wait to be told what to do. By using checklists and receiving positive feedback for completing chores, children learn to help — and to do so independently.

Teachable Moment

By using a checklist, the Shaffer children were able to do what was needed without direction from their parents. Elaine Shaffer introduced the plan one morning when everyone was home until midafternoon. "Here is your checklist with your chores listed," she began. "When you have finished each one, please check it off. When the list says, 'Manager Check,' just come to me, and I'll check your chores to see that they're done right. Then you'll be free to play."

By invoking Grandma's Rule—when you have done what you need to do, then you may do what you want to do—and using a checklist to structure the chores, Lynn and Elaine found that the children not only remembered what needed to be done (a major problem with children who don't include chores in their daily agenda) but also were more willing to do their chores.

Monitor performance and give appropriate feedback. When monitoring the completion of chores, it is important to point out what has been done correctly before telling children what needs to be done to fix mistakes.

WARNING: AVOID REMINDING WHEN CHORES NEED TO BE DONE.

Reminding children of their chores simply makes them dependent and rescues them from the consequences of their lapses. If you let them suffer the consequence of not getting to do what they want to do, children are more likely to be careful about what needs to be done.

Teachable Moment

By praising those things that were done correctly, the Shaffers let their children know that their efforts were appreciated. For example, when she saw how neatly Amy and Arnie had cleaned their rooms, Elaine said, "You really straightened your rooms well this morning. Look how nicely you put your sweaters in your drawers and cleared your desk. Now, when the things are taken out from under the bed and put in the closet where they belong, the whole room will look great." Because they could see progress being made, Amy and Arnold were more willing to correct the things that were not done yet.

Elaine knew that by describing her children's behavior when she praised it, they would remember what her expectations were and would be more willing to live up to them.

Praise helpful behaviors. You want children to behave in helpful ways? Point out such behavior when it happens — don't let it slip by just because it was *right*! If you praise those gestures and describe what is happening, your children will feel proud of the behavior, even if they don't let you know how pleased they feel.

WARNING: AVOID PRAISING THE CHILD.

Praise the behavior rather than the child to help children learn that it is the behavior that is the focus rather than whether they are good or bad boys or girls.

Teachable Moment

Elaine had been nagging Arnold about his messy room, his toys scattered about, his dirty clothes left on the floor of the bathroom, and many other habits that bugged her. She asked him to do some chores, but as often as not, he neglected to do them. One amazing day, she carried a basket of clean laundry into the kitchen, then hurried to the living room so she could catch the beginning of the morning news. When she returned to begin folding the laundry, there was Arnold, busily folding and stacking the clothes on the counter.

Enthusiastically, she beamed, "Thank you so much for helping me fold the laundry. I don't know what I would do without your help!"

Actually, Arnold seemed as pleased as she was. Throughout the day, he helped whenever he could, and he was praised for his effort. Somehow, everything about the day seemed nicer to Elaine after her son's helpfulness. She now was a firm believer in the old adage "You can catch more flies with honey than you can with vinegar."

Model helpful manners. Children who see their parents holding doors for each other, letting others go first, and offering to help see models of the very behaviors parents want their children to imitate. If those behaviors are reinforced with smiles, positive body language, and compliments, children learn the value of such behaviors, as well as how to actually do them.

"My parents taught me to hold the door open for people who can't open it themselves, because it's a nice, polite thing to do." —NICHOLE

Teachable Moment

"Thanks for holding the door for me. That's so helpful of you. You are using such nice manners," Elaine said to

Lynn while they were at the mall. Although she was using the same kind of praise she would use with the children, she wanted to provide a model for them by praising her husband.

"You're welcome, my dear," Lynn answered in similar exaggeration.

Later when they were about to enter another store, Arnie rushed ahead and held the door open for his parents and his sister.

"Arnie, that's so helpful of you. You're so considerate," his parents commented.

By hearing praise for the use of good manners and being helpful, Amy and Arnie learned to think about those behaviors themselves and, over time, made them a part of their repertoire.

Encourage community service. In order to teach your children the value of helping others, involve your family in community service as a vehicle for benefiting the greater community. Most religious organizations have ongoing programs, and many other organizations in cities and towns across the country have developed community service delivery systems looking for volunteers.

Teachable Moment

Both Lynn and Elaine were excited as they received their volunteer assignment from the coordinator. They had been assigned to deliver food this Saturday, food that had been donated to the food pantry to give to people in need.

"But I wanted to play with my friends," Arnold whined.

"Yes, I know you would like to be with your friends on Saturday, but this is important," Elaine replied.

"Yes, Arnie," Lynn continued, "helping others is very

important work. This gives us the chance to help our town and those people who don't have as much as we do."

"But I don't want to go," Arnie complained.

"Well, we've already made arrangements, and we are *all* going," Elaine said firmly.

That Saturday, they arrived at the food pantry and began loading the food bags. Arnold was petulant and didn't want to help. His cheerful and pleasant sister was being praised by her parents for her efforts and jovial spirits.

"Thank you for all your help, Amy," Lynn said as she carried a small bag of food to the car. "I'm sure the people who get this food will appreciate your efforts."

After a while, Arnold began carrying things, and he, too, was praised. "I know you didn't want to come today, but you are being a good sport about it and helping anyway," Elaine told him. "I'm sure you'll feel better when you get to see how helpful your work is to our hungry neighbors."

By the time the day was over, the children were quiet but seemed satisfied with their day. "Do you remember that little boy we saw?" Arnold said. "He was so happy when he saw the peanut butter in the bag. He said he hadn't had peanut butter for a long, long time. I can't even think what it would be like without peanut butter, can you?"

"No," Amy answered. "I can't think what we'd do without peanut butter. I never thought about anyone *not* having it before."

"Life's most persistent and urgent question is: What are you doing for others?" —MARTIN LUTHER KING, JR.

3

FAIRNESS

"Our deeds determine us, as much as we determine our deeds." —GEORGE ELIOT

fair *n.* **1.** free from bias, dishonesty, or injustice **2.** legitimately sought, pursued, done, given, etc.; proper under the rules

- "It wouldn't be fair for me to take the last piece of cake. I'll divide it so we can share it."

- "We need to play the game by the rules. It isn't fair when we keep changing them."

- "It's not fair for you to help with this homework project. Our teacher wants us to do our own work."

- "If we try to make things fair, then we won't get into fights about things not being fair."

CAN LIFE REALLY BE fair? Not in the age-old sense of the word, when it meant "even." Parents today know that "being fair" has taken on a new meaning—an improved one, at that, especially as it relates to child-rearing. Being fair to one's children doesn't mean treating them "equally," because fairness is truly in the eyes (and mind) of the beholder. If fairness benefits only oneself, the definition most children use, then others may end up suffering. But in the world of strong character and caring, a "fair" person is one who can get along with others because he is interested in *everyone* receiving a "fair" deal. The adage "None of us is as smart as all of us" rings true — we all win when everyone feels he contributed and benefited equally.

What Do We Mean by Fairness?

- Fairness means going beyond the letter of agreements and rules to consider what is best for all involved.
- In order to be fair, children must believe that the needs or wants of another person are worth considering, along with their own.
- To want to cooperate, children must be able to put themselves in another person's place and work out "deals" so that everyone believes that he has been heard and dealt a hand he can tolerate.
- To be fair, children must care about the welfare of another person and overcome their own tendency to be selfish.

Meet the Smith Family

Seven-year-old Corey Smith and his five-year-old brother, Jeremy, were rarely concerned about each other's welfare. When one of them tattled on the other, saying he wasn't "being fair," the response often was a vehement "It's fair to me."

Where was the voice of cooperation? Their parents, Wendel and Diane, understood the need for making that voice heard, so that their children could comfortably learn how to engage in rewarding friendships and amiable relationships with their teachers, family, and peers. The Smiths knew that they had to teach Corey and Jeremy not only how to try to make the world a place that was more fair to all but also to accept the fact that what they considered fair for themselves might not be seen as fair by others.

TEACHING TOOLS

Model fairness. In order for your children to best understand the concept of fairness, it is vital to watch your own behavior and try to be as fair as possible with friends, neighbors, family, and even strangers, such as store clerks and those standing near you in waiting lines. By thinking about the welfare of others and keeping in mind what is best for all, you will generally come up with behaviors that can be considered fair. Then point out your appropriate model of behavior when it occurs so that your children can see how striving for fairness helps everyone win.

WARNING: AVOID WEIGHING AND MEASURING EVERYTHING TO ENSURE FAIRNESS.

Many parents try so hard to make things fair that they end up creating more of a problem than they solve. If absolute fairness is the goal, children won't learn to accept situations in which fairness cannot be had. Remember, "fairness" does not mean "equality"; it means cooperating to meet the needs of both parties, and caring about that as a goal in relationships, realizing that different individuals have conflicting needs and wants. Sometimes, in fact, Wendel's being fair can mean that he has such a great sense of empathy for Diane that he knows it's best for *her* desires to be met instead of his own.

Teachable Moment

Wendel Smith walked into the kitchen while Corey and Jeremy were cooperating with each other so that each could have a "fair share" of the breakfast cereal.

"Dad, we're making our own breakfast," Corey said as he saw him. "Do you want some toast? You can have this one. It's the last piece, but we can make some more."

Wendel nearly fainted with surprise. What a good feeling he had from knowing that his children were learning to be fair. Quickly, he recovered from his euphoria, knowing that a compliment was in order. "Thank you for letting me have the last piece of toast. That was very fair of you to think about me," he answered, smiling. "I saw how you were dividing up the cereal so that you could each have some, too," he added. "That was nice of you both to think of each other so things would be fair."

Wendel and Diane not only pointed out fairness when they saw it practiced by their children but also took every opportunity to demonstrate fairness themselves.

"Thanks for helping me clean up the kitchen," Diane told Wendel when they sat down with their children after dinner.

"It's only fair that I help. After all, we both have jobs outside our home, so I think it's fair that we both work around the house, too," Wendel answered, feeling good about his sharing chores with his wife, and helping Corey and Jeremy learn that fairness enables everyone's life to run more smoothly.

Model selflessness. To increase their sense of fairness, children must overcome their tendency toward selfishness and their inclination to think only of their own needs. To help them understand the importance of thinking of others rather than thinking only of themselves, model selflessness for your children by diligently looking for your own self-centered behavior and changing to caring about the welfare of others.

Teachable Moment

Diane was tired. She had worked all day and only wanted some peace and quiet. But she knew that her children needed her attention. She dreaded sitting with them and listening to them tell about their school day, because she was so tired, but she knew that it was important to them.

In spite of herself, she heard these words pouring out of her mouth: "I'm tired. Find something else to do!" When she saw the hurt look on her children's faces, she knew that she had to overcome her own selfish guarding of her time and energy and give her children what they needed.

"I'm sorry. I was only thinking of my needs and not of what was best for you. Tell me now, what good things happened today?" she asked.

As the children excitedly told of their day, Diane felt proud of herself for giving this time to them. After all, she thought, they aren't going to be around forever. She knew it was more important for her to pay attention to them than it was to start dinner. They would manage to get dinner together, she told herself, but no one could do this "listening job" better than she could.

"When I was in first grade I think I learned to be fair. Someone cut in front of me in line, so I pinched her. The next day my parents had the girl over so we could play. They said I had to learn to play fair with other people." — MEGAN

Encourage giving. To help children understand what fairness means, it is important to encourage them to give to others who may be less fortunate. The spirit of giving addresses fairness and selflessness as well as empathy for others. Make the traditional December holidays, as well as other special days, different by making them *giving* days instead of just *getting* days. At these times, volunteer your time and energy to charitable organizations that directly help people. In addition, ask your children to give one of their possessions to a charity at each birthday so that someone less fortunate can have a happy birthday, too. Your children will be rewarded — inside — for helping someone feel so good.

Teachable Moment

"But why should I give up one of my toys on my birthday?" whined five-year-old Jeremy as he was being briefed about the rules governing his upcoming sixth birthday.

"You need to give something to people who don't have many toys, because you have so many. It's only fair that we share what we have with others," Wendel answered patiently.

"You remember the children you met at the homeless shelter two weeks ago when we were there on Sunday serving dinner?" Diane asked. When Jeremy nodded, she continued, "Well, they were children who don't have toys anymore. They don't even have a home to live in. We'll take the toy you decide to give, and the people at the shelter will choose some child who needs a toy and give it to him."

"Because they don't have a home, can they come here and live with us? We have lots of room," Jeremy said, now caught up in the spirit of giving to others.

"That's what the shelter does, sweetheart," Diane answered, smiling. "That's their home now until they find a home of their own. What toy do you think you'll give?"

"I don't know yet," Jeremy answered pensively. "I'll have to think about that for a while. I'll think of one of the kids at the shelter. That'll help me decide."

The Smiths were pleased that Jeremy could see the wisdom of helping others so that the world could be more fair. And on his birthday, they complimented him by saying, "Happy birthday, sweetheart! I hope this will be a special day for you. I'm sure some other child will enjoy the toy you chose to give him as much as you did. It is only fair that we share what we have with others, so that they can have fun, too."

Discourage complaining. When children complain, they are considering only themselves and not what is important to others. By demanding fairness through complaining, they are also devoting their time and energy to things they generally can't control. To help them think of others and to accept the things they can't change, encourage your children to shift their focus to the more positive (partly sunny) side of life, and increase the cost of their keeping the negative (partly cloudy) view in sight.

WARNING: AVOID PUNISHING.

Children who are punished for their lack of fairness only learn to resent the situation and all those associated with it. Punishment doesn't teach the behaviors we want children to learn.

Teachable Moment

"Corey won't let me watch what I want to on TV," Jeremy complained loudly. "It's not fair. He gets to do everything he wants because he's older, and I never get to do what I want."

"It sounds like you think you're getting a bad deal," Wendel answered. "What do you think we should do about your problem?"

Jeremy quickly got to the core of his argument. "Tell him to let me watch what I want."

"But if I make him do what you want, will he think that's fair?" Wendel countered. "And besides, how much TV have you watched today already?"

"Not that much," Jeremy answered. "I've only been watching since six this morning."

"But it's ten now. That's four hours of cartoons. And here you are complaining that you didn't ever get to do what you want." Wendel was on a roll now. "Rather than complain about what you don't have and demand more, let's think of what we do have. Get a pencil and some paper. I want to make a list."

When Jeremy brought the pencil and paper, they started their list. "Let's make a list of all the good things that have happened so far today."

"Well . . . I got to watch cartoons," Jeremy began. "And I got to eat breakfast while I watched on the kitchen TV. And I ate two bowls of my very favorite cereal. And when I get dressed, I get to go play with Drew next door. And . . ." he started, but that was all he could think of.

"Well, Jeremy," Wendel said, "how do you feel now?

Are you still mad because you didn't get to watch more TV?"

"No," he answered. "I guess I'd better get dressed. I want to go play with Drew."

"Instead of doing all that complaining, just think about all the good things that have happened today. But if you choose to complain about things and waste your energy in that way, you will have to do it by yourself in your room," Wendel concluded.

"Okay, Dad," Jeremy answered as he bounded for his room. He was already focused on his plans for the day. Complaining was the farthest thing from his mind now.

Build problem-solving. Children who learn to face problems as they occur and try to find solutions to those problems generally come to accept the world as a fair place, which makes them more likely to collaborate with others. To teach problem-solving, first define the problem. Once the problem is defined, list as many feasible solutions as possible with no attempt to evaluate the worthiness of each solution. When the list of solutions is made, explore the potential consequences of each solution. Finally, choose the best solution based on its being the one with the best possible outcome.

Teachable Moment

"It's not fair that I have to do chores while Corey goes to T-ball practice on Saturday," Jeremy complained as he worked at his assigned chores.

"I understand you don't think it's fair that you have to help with cleaning this Saturday while your brother goes to play ball. Because you see this as a problem, what do you think could be done to make the situation more fair?" Diane asked.

"I think I should get to take the day off or maybe Corey could do the cleaning next Saturday while I go to a friend's to play," Jeremy answered.

"Well, if you take the day off, what do you think will happen? Think about what's best for everybody," Diane suggested.

"I don't know." Jeremy's brow furrowed as he thought. "I guess you'd have to do all the work. That wouldn't be very fair either. Maybe having Corey do all the work next Saturday would be the best."

"How do you suppose he'll feel about that?" Diane continued.

"I guess he won't think that's very fair. But it really is because he didn't do his work today," Jeremy answered. "Maybe you'll have to talk to him like this so he'll understand."

Diane was pleased that her young son was able to think through the problem and to consider the outcomes. The one he reached was fair—because it treated everyone's time with respect.

Mediate television. Children who watch a lot of television begin to think they should have everything they see being advertised or used. When they start wanting everything, they begin to believe it's not fair when they don't get what they want. They begin to focus only on themselves—what they want when they want it—ignoring whether or not their requests are reasonable. In order to help your children learn to delay gratification and understand that TV continually exposes them to things they'll want but can't have, first reduce the amount of time they spend watching TV, and then problem-solve with them to help them think through positive ways to possibly get what they want.

WARNING: AVOID LECTURING.

Children only learn how not to listen when we lecture them. Trying to say the same thing to them in many different ways doesn't teach them the behaviors we want them to learn.

Teachable Moment

"Everybody has this new video game, Nanuck, with great graphics, and all I have is this stupid thing," Corey complained as he sat in front of the TV pointing at his now-antiquated video game. "They just advertised Nanuck on TV, and it's really cool. Can we get it? Please! Please! Please!" Corey was insistent.

"I'm sorry you can't have everything you see on TV that you want. I'll tell you what, though; let's see if we can find a solution to this problem," Diane answered. "Maybe we could figure out a way that you could earn the game."

"But I want it now!" Corey whined.

"Well, I'm sorry you can't have what you want the minute you want it. The only way you will be able to have it is if you earn it," Diane continued, now more forcefully. "So you decide; work for it or do without."

"What will I have to do?" Corey asked, looking petulant.

"Well, I need to talk to your dad about this first. So I'll tell you what we'll do. Your dad and I'll make a list of jobs that need to be done and how much they're worth. Then you can decide what you want to do. Okay?"

"I guess. When can I know?"

"We'll try to talk about it tonight, but I think you can be patient. I know it's hard, but you can do it."

Later that evening, when she and Wendel had time to talk about Corey's request, they first decided that they needed to cut back on the time the kids spent watching TV. Then, the next evening, Diane and Wendel sat down with the boys and went through the TV listings. Together they decided what they would watch for the next week. Both boys were upset that they couldn't watch anytime they wanted, but after a few days, they learned to play outside again and even talk more with their parents and each other. Without the exposure to the "toy store" on television, the demands for toys and other things advertised on TV began to drop. Even after the list was created, Corey decided that the Nanuck game wasn't that important to him when he knew that he had to work to get it.

"I say that justice is truth in action." —BENJAMIN DISRAELI

4

TOLERANCE

"Toleration is good for all, or it is good for none."
— EDMUND BURKE

tol·er·ance *n.* 1. a fair and objective attitude toward those whose opinions, practices, race, religion, nationality, or the like differ from one's own; freedom from bigotry 2. any liberal, undogmatic viewpoint 3. the act or capacity of enduring; endurance

- "Mommy! I don't really like peas, but they're okay."

- "Today at school, the kids were making fun of Molly. I told them that was wrong."

- "I don't like the way my teacher favors the girls, but I guess I can stand it."

- "It's not that I hate my sister. It's just that she's always around. I'd like to have some time by myself just to hang out when she isn't here."

IT SEEMS TO BE a commonly understood theme among parent-to-parent conversations today: More and more children seem to have a cynical, disrespectful, and intolerant attitude toward others and behave as if they are absolutely entitled to everything they want to have, say, or do, whenever they want to have, say, or do it. In fact, if they don't want to make any effort to understand or accept others, because it frustrates them to do so, they believe they are entitled to not have to make that effort.

So how can a parent teach his children to do the mental work necessary to understand and endure — tolerate — the people and activities around them that are different from themselves? First he must teach them to tolerate the frustration that often comes with effort. This work may take some "mental muscle" that may be undeveloped, but strengthening that muscle is critically important because it teaches children how to get along in an increasingly diverse world of work and play.

WHAT DO WE MEAN BY TOLERANCE?

- Tolerance means giving to others with no expectation of anything in return.
- Tolerating frustration means being willing to make the effort required to do things that are difficult.
- Understanding the position of another person and appreciating the similarities and differences help create tolerant attitudes.
- Being tolerant means reducing the destructive nature of competition — being able "to stand it" if one loses.
- Being empathic and caring toward others is a sign of tolerance.

MEET THE BROWN FAMILY

Alexis, aged ten, and Jane, eight, talked to each other as if they couldn't stand the sight of the other. Their tolerance level was so low that their parents, Jim and Beth, thought that they might have to keep them in separate parts of the house until they were grown! Verbal ammunition, such as "I can't stand the sight of you!" "You're too stupid to live!" and "How can anyone stand to be around you — you're so gross!" was constantly being shot as everyday conversation.

Jim and Beth wondered, "Do our children actually *want* to hurt each other's feelings?" They believed that their children were putting each other down without realizing that this verbal slugfest was wounding their relationship and general attitude about life — and everything in it.

Because the television programs, playground games, and soccer fields reverberated with these sharp remarks, Jim and Beth knew that they would need lots of opportunity to change the choices of words their children used. Even at their young ages, the peer pressure was strong to cling to their put-downs as a defense against arrows shot their way.

"I think it is very important to learn to tolerate others, because eventually there is going to be someone you don't like, and there will be nothing you can do about it." — MEGAN

TEACHING TOOLS

Help children tolerate teasing. Within the "game" of sibling rivalry, there can be lots of teasing and put-downs as the players vie for higher status in the eyes of their parents. These attacks between siblings can become vicious enough to result in physical as well as emotional damage, as the participants express their lack of tolerance for the very existence of a brother or sister. Sometimes, a child whose self-esteem has become particularly low as a result of the mental and physical abuse by a sibling bullies others at school and in the neighborhood as he uses the same abusive tactics to improve his own status.

To avoid the potential damage sibling rivalry can cause, it is important to be alert to intolerant words and actions as children interact. At the first sign of abusive intolerance, refocus the abuser on getting along and help him develop tolerance for his sibling's family membership. Support the victim of intolerance by helping him use empathy to understand who owns the problems and why.

WARNING: AVOID ATTACKING THE "PERSON."

Frequently, when angry or frustrated by behavior in children, parents resort to character assassination. Keep the behavior in mind when you discipline, because it is the *behavior* that can change and it is the *behavior* that you want to change.

Teachable Moment

One morning at breakfast, the sour sounds of sibling quibbling emanated from the kitchen. As Beth approached, she heard Alexis say, "I can't stand the sight of your ugly face. Turn your back to me before I throw up."

"I hate your ugly face, too," screamed her sister in retaliation.

"I'm sorry you two are choosing not to get along this morning," Beth began as she entered the kitchen. She knew she shouldn't try to get to the bottom of the problem, because that would just increase the conflict.

"But she started it," Jane began, but Beth cut her short.

"It doesn't matter who started what. That sort of talk is very hurtful and will not be tolerated in this house. I want you to get along with each other. We are a family and getting along is important."

"Well, I try to get along, but . . ." Alexis said.

"Yes, I understand that you both feel that the other deserves what she gets, but you need to think about how your sister must feel when you say things like that. It must really hurt her feelings," Beth continued. "I want you two to get along. As long as you can do that, you can do what you want to do. If you can't get along, then you'll work for me. Doing something constructive is a much better use of family time than doing something destructive."

Throughout the day, Beth made it a point to compliment her daughters when they were getting along. "Thank you for getting along," she would say, even if they were just coexisting in the same room. And that night as she sat with Jane as a part of her bedtime routine, her daughter asked a very difficult question.

"Mom, why does Alexis hate me so much?"

"I don't think she really hates you," her mom began. "You see, she was in our family first, and I think she doesn't always like it because she has to share with you. She may really be mad at your dad and me because it was our choice to bring you into our family. But she can't beat up on *us*, so *you're* it." Beth then tried to help Jane with some tease tolerance. "When Alexis is being really mean, what do you suppose you could do?"

As they worked through the potential solutions and consequences, Jane decided to tell her sister how much her words hurt by saying, "That hurts my feelings, and I don't like it when you say that," and walking away from her. That would leave Alexis' verbal shots right where they belonged — out of the game. In this way, Jane would see Alexis "lose points" as she kept making unproductive, illegal shots, and Jane would not blame herself for having caused her sister's "faulty" behavior.

Mediate television. Is there a monster swallowing up the manners, positive attitude, and compassion toward others in your home? The monster is the television if it is turned on to programs that contain language that puts others down and story lines that are based on intolerance of others. Children can learn these inappropriate lessons as easily as ones about the positive ways to live life. In order to know what influences their behavior, sit with your children while they watch their favorite programs. Be aware of the humor that characters use to put others down or demean others because of their particular looks or behavior. Look for sexist or racist remarks, or stereotyping of ethnic or particular physical characteristics. Comment on these discoveries during commercials and after the show by posing questions to your children about the behavior. This launching pad for a discussion helps you understand how your children interpreted the characters' dialogue and actions.

WARNING: AVOID USING PUT-DOWNS.

Sometimes people will put others down in an attempt to be funny, as so many comedians do. In fact, much of comedy that is on television or in movies is simply a string of put-downs. In real life, however, there is no audience laughter and those put-downs take their toll, sending the message that there isn't much tolerance for others in the world.

Teachable Moment

The Browns began to notice certain comments and phrases that were creeping into their daughters' vocabulary which not only were unkind but also reflected a level of intolerance. They also recognized some of the phrases as those coming from a television program they knew the girls were watching.

"Don't have a cow, man!" Jane said to Jim when he turned off the television because it was dinnertime.

"Wow! Where'd you learn to talk like that?" Jim asked his daughter.

"That's how they talk on TV," Jane answered calmly.

"Well, it's not appropriate language in our home," Jim countered. "I don't like the idea that you're learning to talk like an insulting, intolerant TV character. I guess we need to watch programs with you so we can see what you're learning."

Beginning then, Jim and Beth monitored the TV viewing of their daughters. What they discovered was a wealth of inappropriate and intolerant situations and language. They asked a lot of questions when they saw things that they considered inappropriate.

"What would you feel like if someone said that to you? Are those guys on the show tolerating each other?" Beth asked her daughters as they watched TV.

"I don't think I'd like it," Alexis answered.

"Why do you suppose they say things like that on TV when people wouldn't like to be talked to like that?" Beth continued.

"I don't know. It's kind of dumb to talk to people so they get their feelings hurt," Alexis answered.

After several weeks of monitored TV, the family decided that reading might be more fun to do during the family's entertainment hours. Jim and Beth noted a decrease in put-downs and cute phrases that were designed to be funny but were exposed as the insensitive, hurtful assault weapons they were.

"My mom and dad always told me to be patient with my brother and sister when they were younger and always got into stuff when they felt like it." —JOYCE

Encourage giving. Children learn about how to be more tolerant of others when they take on the others' role. Establishing an outreach program for your family is one way children can learn to care about and to give of themselves to others in an organized fashion. Working in a soup kitchen, donating toys, food, and clothing to a homeless shelter, and volunteering in a nursing home are only a few of the ways to encourage children to experience the rewards of giving to others.

Teachable Moment

The Browns began volunteering their time in a mission that was frequented by unemployed people. Every Sunday, they would take Alexis and Jane and help serve dinner with other community volunteers. At first, the girls were reluctant to leave the safety of the kitchen, but with encouragement and in the company of a parent, they ventured among the recipients of their good work. Afterward, the family would discuss how they felt and what they learned during their trips to the mission. The girls admitted feeling quite different toward the people who couldn't find work after a few weeks, and both asked what more they could do to help people who were less fortunate than they were.

Study others' cultures and ways. Children tend to be less tolerant of those whom they don't understand. Studying other cultures is one way to help your children debunk the myths they've heard about those who seem strange to them.

When they learn the reasons for others' dress, habits, etc., it becomes clear that their styles and rituals have value just as one's own do. Visiting ethnic festivals and other churches are only two of the many ways to help your children be familiar with different people's way of life in our increasingly diverse society.

Teachable Moment

The Browns decided that they should help Alexis and Jane understand better their classmates' backgrounds.

"Who in your class is of a different race from you? Who in your class is of a different religion?" were questions they asked their children.

Over the next several weeks, the girls made a list of the different races and religions in their classes. Then their parents suggested that they visit a church on Sunday that was of a different religion than theirs and was made up mostly of people of a different race. Afterward, they talked about what they had seen that was different and what was the same. By receiving this brief personal experience of hearing the music and conversation of some of their classmates' culture, the girls admitted that they were more comfortable and accepting of their not-so-foreign ways.

Help children understand that "different" isn't "bad."
Many children think that someone is "wrong" if he doesn't think or act the way they do. Help your children realize that being different is a fact of life. Even older children can benefit from a little lesson of the world of genetics and personality. By understanding where another person's

ideas and beliefs come from, a child can develop an *appreciation* for them as well as tolerance and empathy.

WARNING: AVOID PRACTICING PREJUDICE.

Many people inadvertently convey their prejudices to others in what they say. Making comments about people's weight, color, height, gender, clothing, or anything else that would convey less tolerance for differences should be avoided.

Teachable Moment

Alexis came home from school one day and said, "There's this new boy in my class, Joe, who doesn't speak English very well. His clothes are kind of old and ragged — everybody stayed away from him."

Jim then asked, "If that boy looks and acts differently from you, is that bad? Does that make him somebody you won't want to be around? Are you afraid of people who are different?"

After discussing the whys and wherefores of Joe for a while, Alexis decided that she should try to learn more about him. She understood how he must feel, being the new boy in class and not understanding what people were saying. Her newly found empathy allowed her to feel what it must be like to be a new person in a strange place — a situation she had been in when she went to preschool for the first time and when she first joined her softball team. Being able to relate his situation to her own life helped both Joe and Alexis begin a conversation and allowed Alexis to learn more about him — his family and the country in which he used to live. A friendship, based on mutual respect for each other's differences, blossomed naturally between the two children.

"You need patience first, to acquire toleration."
— RACHEL

Reinforce standing up for the rights of others. When children are taught that everyone has rights that must be protected, they are more likely to believe that someone should stand up for those rights. Discussing the rights people have and trying to apply those rights to what's viewed on television, in the movies, at school, or even on the playground help encourage children to be more aware of ways to protect the rights of everyone.

Teachable Moment

At dinner, Jane told her family about Dan, a classmate who was being picked on by other students because he was considered to be a pest. Jane had defended him to her classmates, but she was now afraid that the others would turn on her.

"That was kind of you, Jane, to have defended Dan like that," Beth gently answered. "I'm sure he felt good to know that someone cared about his rights. But what can you do if some of the others start teasing you about defending him?"

After playing the role of teaser and victim, Jane came to the conclusion that she could tolerate some criticism and still feel okay about herself. She decided that she could simply say, "I don't like it when you talk to me like that," and walk away from the critic. That would send the message that she wasn't going to tolerate unkindness in any form.

"Though all society is founded on intolerance, all improvement is founded on tolerance." — GEORGE BERNARD SHAW

5

CARING

"The quality of mercy is not strained;/It droppeth as the gentle rain from heaven/Upon the place beneath; it is twice blessed;/It blesseth him that gives and him that takes." — WILLIAM SHAKESPEARE

> care *vb*. 1. to feel interest or concern 2. to give care (for the sick) *n*. 1. a sense of responsibility 2. painstaking or watchful attention 3. regard coming from desire or esteem

- "Why does that man have one leg, Mommy? I feel sorry for him."
- "My friend Mary got hurt today on the playground. Can I call and see how she is?"
- "Mrs. Brown needs some help with her yard. I'm going to help her on Saturday."
- "It's so unfair when kids call names. It's like they don't care how other people feel."

MUSIC. DANCE. ART. CARING. What do all of these have in common? Each activity uses the soul as its fuel, its energy. Caring is a particularly rewarding skill to develop because it has the benefit of creating immediate feedback and rewards. The amazing fact about caring is that, as mystical a force as it is, it still must be actively taught and modeled in order to become part of a person's principles of living. A baby does not genetically receive the knowledge of how to be a caring person from his parents. However, through the teachable moments that offer positive feedback for caring about others, a child learns that it not only is emotionally rewarding for him to be a caring person but also is of great benefit to the recipient of caring.

Even though developmentally, most very young children are capable of thinking primarily of themselves, they are also capable of caring about others and feeling empathy. If parents and other significant adults are not readily available to reinforce and acknowledge caring during these formative years, however, young children can grow up without any understanding of the impact they have on others. They may learn to bully, to demand from others, to remain self-centered, and to think nothing of unkindness primarily because they haven't been taught otherwise.

"Knowing that everyone has feelings makes it a lot easier to care about someone." — MEGAN

WHAT DO WE MEAN BY CARING?

- Caring means having the ability to think about the needs and feelings of others.
- Caring people have the ability to project themselves into the role of another person.
- Caring requires the ability to experience empathy.
- In order to demonstrate caring behavior, a person might have to defer his needs in order to help another first.

Meet the Cascio Family

Michael and Mary Cascio were concerned that their children might not acquire the ability to care about the needs of others because on a daily basis they witnessed their fighting with each other, competing for territory, bullying, arguing, and generally behaving in ways that were uncaring and selfish. The oldest, ten-year-old Sean, was angry, argumentative, and bossy. His eight-year-old sister, Martha, fought back and, in turn, frequently verbally attacked six-year-old Megan. The youngest, four-year-old Ryan, was the loudest, most demanding of the bunch; occasionally Mary was tempted to hire a baby-sitter for him even if she was going to be home!

Teaching Tools

Teach and reinforce empathy. During the preschool years, children are fully capable of caring about others' feelings; but for them to continue to have empathy for others, they must be told how their behavior affects others. So when your children begin to say things or act in ways that will hurt others, immediately explain how their behavior makes their victims feel. Relate those feelings to times when you know someone has hurt *them*, too, to remind them of their own experience of being hurt by others.

WARNING: AVOID OVERREACTING TO YOUR CHILD'S UN-CARING ACTS.

Until they learn to care about the feelings and needs of others, your children may often treat others unkindly.

Overreacting to unkindness will reinforce the idea that your child is bad. Once he decides that he is bad, he might become resigned to that fact, and being a "bad person" might become a self-fulfilling prophecy.

Teachable Moment

Ryan had been whining and demanding all morning, and Mary was just about at the end of her rope. When he demanded something to drink and started screaming when the drink wasn't to his liking, she was about to scream back at him but decided to just turn away and leave him in the kitchen alone. She was filling her mind with words like *smooth, calm, quiet,* and *soft* in order to ease her anger. When she felt calmer, she went back to Ryan, who was now sitting on the floor of the kitchen with tears running down his face.

She calmly looked directly at him and said, "I feel really hurt inside when you yell and scream like that. I'm sure you wouldn't like for me to yell and scream at you like that. From now on when you do that, you'll go to time-out," she informed him. (Time-out means to be without reinforcement from children or adults during a set period of time, generally one minute for each year of age. Time-out can be on a chair, in a corner, or in a child's room with the door closed.)

Ryan gave her a puzzled look and then, as a test, he began screaming at her again.

"I told you that hurts my feelings when you do that, so now you'll go to time-out," she replied, pulling off his shoes and putting him in his room with the door closed. Ryan was really angry, so he kicked the door; he quickly realized, though, that without shoes, kicking the door wasn't a good idea!

When time-out was over, Mary and Ryan talked for a few minutes about how they would all get along better if he thought about how others might feel before he decided how to behave. After a few weeks, she noted Ryan stopping himself — almost in midtantrum — before he hurt his friend's or his family's feelings with his words and actions.

Model caring and empathy. Because caring and empathy are abstract concepts, adults must show children how to behave in caring and empathic ways. By *seeing* how to behave, children will learn the behaviors of caring and empathy more quickly than if parents just tell them.

WARNING: AVOID DEMEANING YOUR CHILD'S CHARACTER.

Telling your child that he is bad for being unkind will only reinforce his belief that he, indeed, is a bad person. The problem of a lack of caring doesn't lie in your child's character, but rather in his behavior — and the behavior can be changed.

Teachable Moment

Mike and Mary realized that they had just been *telling* their children to "behave," not showing them what they meant by that. So when Martha began complaining about something being unfair, Mike decided to demonstrate what "being caring" really meant in specific words. He answered her by saying, "I'm sorry you are feeling bad. Is there anything I can do to help?"

"It's not fair that Sean gets to go to a friend's on Saturday, and I have to go with you and Mom to shop for things. I want to stay home. I'm big enough," she whined.

"I'm sorry you can't always do what you want. I know

you don't like to go shopping with Mom and me and the other kids. I wish we could let you stay home."

"You could let me stay if you wanted! You're just being mean!" Martha yelled.

"It really hurts my feelings when you talk to me like that!" her father answered calmly. "Here I was being nice to you, and you treated me badly. It makes me feel sad that you don't care about my feelings."

"I'm sorry, Daddy. I didn't mean to yell," Martha apologized, and she began to cry.

"Thank you for saying you're sorry. Because I care so much about how you feel, we'll try to do something nice together while we're out shopping," Mike said as he held his young daughter in his arms to comfort her.

Mediate television. Your children can learn a lot from watching TV; but that education may not be all about caring and empathy. When you watch what your children are watching, it gives you the opportunity to talk about situations in which the characters are mean and hurtful to each other. In addition, watching the programs with them allows you to point out alternative ways that the characters *could* have chosen to act — ways that you hope your children will model.

Teachable Moment

After deciding that she really needed to know what television programs her children were watching, Mary sat down with them one afternoon when they were out of school. She was appalled as she listened to the cartoon character in the show talk to his father in very uncaring ways. It was as if this little boy cared only for himself and his own wants and needs, and the needs of the other family members were of no importance.

"What do you think about what Supersam just said to his father?" Mary asked her children.

"I think it's funny!" Sean answered with a laugh, and the others chorused their agreement.

"What if you talked to Dad that way?" she continued. "Would that be funny, too?"

Sean turned and looked at his mother. "I don't think so . . ."

"How do you think Dad would like it if you talked that way?" she pushed on.

"Daddy would be mad. He'd say his feelings were hurt," Martha chimed in, remembering her recent conversation with her father.

"Why do you suppose Dad would have hurt feelings?" Mary asked.

"Because talking to people like that isn't a kind thing to do," Sean said, frowning.

"I guess it wouldn't be very nice if we all talked to each other like that, would it?" Mary concluded.

After that conversation, the family had two or three more discussions about that particular program. Within the next week, she noticed that her children didn't enjoy that program as much anymore, and eventually, they stopped watching it altogether.

Stay close to and supervise play activities. While your young children play with each other or other children, it is important to monitor their play to ensure caring behavior. In the event that you hear or see behavior that reflects a lack of kindness and caring, it is important to intervene quickly by stopping the activity, then pointing out the effect of the unkindness and suggesting alternative ways of behaving or of resolving a conflict.

WARNING: AVOID LECTURING.

As tempting as it may be to explain in a variety of ways why caring is good and not caring is bad, long lectures only teach children to tune out adults. Rather than lecture, ask your children questions that will help lead them to the conclusion you would like them to have.

Teachable Moment

Mary was working in her kitchen as Ryan and his young playmate were playing in the next room. She heard her son call his friend Jimmy a dummy. When she went in to see what was going on, she saw that Ryan was raising his fist to haul off and clobber Jimmy.

"Ryan! What's the rule about hitting?" Mom asked.

"He wouldn't play what I wanted to play!" Ryan answered plaintively.

"Because someone doesn't do exactly what we want, is that any reason to call names and hit?" his mother calmly asked.

"I guess not," reluctantly came the answer from Ryan.

"How do you think Jimmy felt when you called him a dummy and threatened to hit him?" she asked her son.

"He didn't like it, I guess."

"What could you have done instead of calling names and threatening to hit?"

"I don't know," Ryan answered.

"Jimmy, what would you like for Ryan to do when he wants you to play what he wants?" she asked his playmate.

"I'd like for him to ask me if it's okay to play what he wants, and if I don't want to do it, then let me play what *I* want. And when he's at my house, he'll get to pick," Jimmy answered thoughtfully.

"What do you think, Ryan?" she asked. "Would that be a good way to solve this problem?"

When Ryan answered that it would, she then suggested that they all practice a few times so that she could be sure they knew how to get along according to these new rules.

"Even though you learned caring when you were little, you need it all through life because caring for others does not necessarily mean caring for just people. It means caring for every living thing and the things they care for." — RACHEL

Make community service a family routine. Your children will learn to care about others while in the practice of community service. Volunteering time to help others will not only help your children understand how their actions can be of positive benefit to people but also help them learn empathy, overcome egocentricity, improve self-esteem, and increase family solidarity.

Teachable Moment

When their dad and mom announced that the family would be spending part of Saturday working in a church-sponsored soup kitchen for new immigrants, all of the children rebelled, in unison.

"But I wanted to play soccer with my friends," whined Sean.

"I was going to Sara's and her mom was going to take us to the shopping center so we could look at dolls and stuff," wailed the indignant Martha.

"I don't like people who talk funny. They scare me," Megan announced in her concrete, six-year-old way.

"I'm not going! I'm not going! I'm not going . . ." chanted Ryan, who could give no specific reason, but loved to echo his siblings.

"I understand this experience may be uncomfortable at first and will take time away from your friends, but it is important for us as a family to do this," Mary said calmly.

"We can always do those other things," their dad continued, "but we can't always help other people. This is our chance to do something for someone else for a change."

The grumbling continued, and when it was time to leave for the soup kitchen on Saturday, the children were angry and sullen. They arrived at their destination, and the children were assigned chores. As the refugees arrived and the children saw that these families were not unlike their own, they began to get into the spirit of the experience. They helped serve food, carried water, filled glasses, brought tableware and napkins, and even helped clean up afterward.

On the way home, they chatted eagerly about their experience and the people they had seen.

"How do you feel now about immigrants to America?" their mom asked, and they all talked at once about how excited and good they felt about what they had done.

Michael and Mary both knew that their children had learned something about caring that Saturday—a life lesson that was as nourishing for their souls as the food they served was to the shelter's diners.

". . .that best portion of a good man's life.
His little, nameless, unremembered acts
Of kindness and of love."
— WILLIAM WORDSWORTH

6

COURAGE

"Life shrinks or expands in proportion to one's courage." — ANAÏS NIN

> **courage** *n.* **1.** the quality of mind or spirit that enables a
> person to face difficulty, danger, pain, etc., with firmness and
> without fear; bravery **Syn.** FEARLESSNESS, DAUNTLESSNESS,
> INTREPIDITY, FORTITUDE, PLUCK, SPIRIT
> **have the courage of one's convictions** *vb.* to act in accor-
> dance with one's beliefs, esp. in spite of criticism

- "I don't care what they think. I like the way I am."

- "Yeah, they were pretty mean to me. But I just told them to leave me alone."

- "I was scared at first. But then I just thought in my head that I could do it."

- "I'm sorry! I was wrong, and I'm not afraid to admit it."

PEER PRESSURE, KEEPING UP with the crowd, teasing — these are some of the battles children face today. They may not need to prepare themselves for the bravery required of soldiers in combat, but they still must face the enemy of fear on these potentially dangerous fronts. Children see murder and mayhem as they watch the evening news; and often at school, in their neighborhoods, and even at home, children are faced with difficult choices which take courage and conviction. To stand up to teasing, to stick to their beliefs in the face of sometimes overwhelming pressure, to be unique when asked to conform, and to admit mistakes to others all take a new definition of courage today.

"My dad said to be brave but not stupid." — JAY

WHAT DO WE MEAN BY COURAGE?

- Taking reasonable risks involves courage.
- When admitting his mistakes, a person shows that he has courage.
- Courage is needed when fighting for one's beliefs.
- Taking pride in being unique calls for courage.
- It takes courage to stand up to teasing.

MEET THE MEISNER FAMILY

Denise Meisner was a single mom with two children, five-year-old Jamie and seven-year-old Mark. Denise was often worried about her ability to teach courage to her two little boys, who rarely heard from their father; this showed a lack of courage on his part, she believed. Her own father was elderly, and her only brother lived many miles away. She wasn't sure how to teach her boys to have courage, without a same-sex role model to help her, but she was determined to try.

TEACHING TOOLS

Model courage. The most important teaching tool parents have is their own behavior. Children are great imitators, so they want to behave as the adults in their lives do. When faced with situations that are frightening, it is important to show courage so that children can see how to handle their own fears.

Teachable Moment

It was well after midnight when the wind began to pick up and the first patter of raindrops could be heard on the window. In the distance was the rumble of thunder, but the rumble rapidly became louder until bangs and booms were rattling the windows and flashes of lightning were making the bedroom as light as if it were midday.

"*Mommeeeeee!*" came Jamie's plaintive cry from the room next door, and Denise knew the little guy was scared.

She was about to get up when the thunder crashed so loudly that the whole house shook. "Wow! That was close," Denise said aloud as her feet hit the floor.

But just then her bedroom door crashed open, and there in the flashbulb light of the storm stood Jamie and Mark. Seeing her, they ran for the bed and burrowed under her covers.

"Hey, guys! Leave some room for me!" Denise yelled over the thunder, and she crawled under the covers with them. They plastered themselves to her as they huddled together listening to the storm. With every clap of thunder, they jumped — they were really scared.

"It's okay, guys. It's only a thunderstorm," she said. "We can handle this. It's going to be okay."

"But, Mom," Jamie's muffled voice came from under the covers, "I'm afraid it'll get us!"

"I know," Denise answered, "but it's only noise. The thunder can't get us, and the lightning mostly strikes tall stuff like trees."

"Yeah, Jamie," Mark said, trying to sound brave. "It's only noise. It can't hurt us."

"You boys are brave and strong and you can handle storms like this," Denise said. "Now, let's try to get some sleep. When you wake up in the morning, you'll see that everything is okay."

They all snuggled together in her big bed, and soon the boys were asleep. Denise lay listening to the storm moving off into the distance. She felt secure with them lying beside her, because she had been as tempted as they were to give in to the fear of the storm. She was happy with herself that she was able to at least present a brave face to them so that they could feel secure and follow her courageous lead.

"Think of something nice when you think there are monsters under the bed." — SARA

Teach children to stand up for their own rights as well as others'. When children learn to stand up for their rights, they are demonstrating the courage of their convictions. The more difficult task, however, is to stand up for the rights of others. When they do so, they are not only sticking to their own principles, they are also putting themselves in the shoes of the other person. To aid your children in learning courage, help them to understand how others feel and to be free to stand up for others' rights against anyone. Help them to be aware that they might suffer as a result of the stand they take—which is an essential part of learning courage. Keep in mind, however, that the old adage "Discretion is the better part of valor" is applicable today. In areas where violence is an automatic reaction to frustration, standing up for others may not be the best choice of behavior. In these cases, avoiding confrontation through "keeping one's distance" is often the best solution.

WARNING: AVOID USING SHAME TO TEACH COURAGE.

Courage is not something we can demand from children. It grows from making a commitment and sticking with it. If you demand courage and shame children for not showing it, they are more likely to resent the demand rather than to choose to be brave. Statements such as "Aren't you ashamed of yourself?" will only create shame and doubt in children rather than foster courage.

Teachable Moment

When Mark described how some of his classmates were picking on his friend at school, Denise asked him what he thought he should do about that. "I guess I should try to make them stop picking on him," Mark answered slowly. "But if I do, then they'll get mad at me."

"That is a problem," Denise replied. "Sometimes our fear of what others might think can stand in the way of standing up for our friends. What choices do you have when the kids pick on other kids?"

Mark thought through the problem and said that he could tell the teacher, try to talk the kids out of being mean, or fight for his friend. He eventually decided that he would feel most comfortable with rescuing his friend or anybody who was being picked on. Somehow, he decided, if it happened again, he and his friend would just choose something else to do, away from the bullies, so they could avoid wasting their time on doing something they knew was wrong — getting into fights.

Denise was proud of Mark for his courage in standing

up for his friend and she told him so. "Mark, you must feel good that you are willing to stand up for your friend even though you know you might suffer. I'm really proud of your courage."

Mark beamed, and Denise knew that he was learning the valuable lesson of courage.

"It's good to stand up for what you believe in."
— ANNIE

Teach children to cope with their own fears. Children naturally develop fears, because they mix a rich fantasy life with the reality around them. Although their fears may seem quite irrational to adults, they are absolutely real to them. Their fears will change as they grow and develop, but they will probably always have some sort of fear, just as all adults usually do. Rather than try to get them to give up their fears, it is better to help them learn to cope with them. To teach coping, allow your children to have their fears, but encourage them to believe that they are brave and strong enough to live through the fear that they feel. In that way, they will learn not to fear the feeling itself, and will be more likely to develop the courage to cope with whatever makes them feel afraid.

Teachable Moment

"Mommy, I'm scared," came this little voice that roused Denise from a deep sleep. "Mommy, I'm scared," the voice said again with greater insistence.

Denise opened one eye and saw the face of her five-year-old only a few inches from hers. "Jamie, what is it?" she mumbled, her head thick with sleep.

"I woke up and heard a noise, and I'm scared," he insisted. "Can I get in bed with you?"

"No, Jamie," she answered softly. "I think it would be better if you could just go back to bed, try to relax, and go back to sleep."

"But, Mommy, I'm afraid something will get me," he continued. "There are noises in the house. Listen, hear that?"

"That's just the house creaking and cracking. Houses do that, because they expand during the day and contract at night when it's cool."

"I don't get it," Jamie answered in a puzzled voice. "It still scares me."

"I understand, sweetie, but nothing will happen to you," Denise insisted. "Now, let's get you back in bed."

Reluctantly, Jamie went back into the room he shared with his brother, Mark, who was still fast asleep. Denise resisted the urge to point out the fact that Mark wasn't afraid. She knew that sort of comparison wouldn't help Jamie much at all. He bounded into bed, and she tucked his covers up under his chin.

"Jamie, you're brave and strong and you can handle being afraid. You'll see! You'll wake up in the morning and everything will be okay. Now tell yourself to think of really fun stuff so that you don't think of bad things. You'll be okay, because you're brave and strong. Good night," and she leaned over and kissed him on the forehead. Her hand was on his chest, and she could feel his pounding heart slow down as he began to relax.

A few weeks later, she casually asked Jamie why he slept with his head under his covers and his body all scrunched up against the wall. "That way the monsters don't get me," he answered matter-of-factly. She knew he was beginning to live with his fears by devising his own system of controlling them. He was developing courage.

Teach courage through problem solving. Children who have learned to think through a problem, develop alternative solutions, analyze the potential consequences of their solution, and pick one that looks best are able to muster the courage to cope with teasing and other emotionally damaging behavior that others shoot their way, because they have learned how to take more control of their reactions to it.

Teachable Moment

Mark came home from school complaining about being called names by two of his most obnoxious, bullying classmates. He was very upset and angry. During dinner, Denise asked him about the problem. "Why do they call you names?"

"I don't know," Mark replied. "I get mad and yell at them, and they just laugh."

"Maybe they just like to see you get mad," Denise suggested.

"I hate them when they do that," Mark said angrily.

"How about trying to come up with something you can do about this problem?" Denise suggested, and she got a piece of paper and a pencil. "Now, let's try to come up with as many different ways of reacting as you can when they call you names."

They began making a list which included such solutions as beat up the kids, tell the teacher, get mad at the kids, and ignore them. Then Denise asked Mark what he thought might happen if he tried each one of the possible solutions. With Denise guiding him, Mark began to reject the violent solutions, because he knew they were wrong and the consequences were too severe. He didn't like to tell the teacher, because that would only give the others another name to call him. He finally decided to try to ignore the bullying, but Denise saw that he was unsure about how to ignore something that upset him so much.

"If you want to ignore them, here's how you can do that. When they call you a name, say 'I don't like it when you say that!' and walk away." Denise suggested. "Now, let's practice to see if it works."

She called him some names, and he said, "I don't like it when you say that!" and walked away from her. "Great!" she yelled. "Now, let's try it again."

This problem-solving and training session taught Mark how to think through problems and to carry out solutions he had decided were useful. Because he now had some new skills, he also had more courage to face the name-calling with confidence.

Help children establish and maintain their own unique-ness. Children need to belong to a peer group, and their strong attachment to this group underlies their thinking that if they are different from others, they won't be accepted by their friends. Being different, then, is seen as dangerous, because children want to fit in and be like everyone else. Helping children recognize and understand their own uniqueness is an important beginning in helping them develop the courage to be themselves, thereby exploding this myth that "different" is unlikable.

Teachable Moment

When they were asked to wear sweaters that Grandmother Brown had sent them, Mark rebelled and Jamie followed suit.

"If I wear this, everybody'll think I'm a geek," Mark cried. "Nobody else wears stuff like this. I'll be different."

"The kids at preschool will make fun of me, too, if I wear that," Jamie joined in.

Instead of dishing out punishment for their obstinate refusal, Denise tossed them some questions.

"So what if you do look different?" she asked. "Is that going to be so bad that you can't stand it? You know what to do if kids make fun of you. We've practiced how to ignore teasing. Grandmother Brown will feel so good when you write to tell her that you wore the sweaters today."

Given this food for thought, Mark and his brother saw their behavior in a new light — the light of deciding one's choices of behavior based on one's own principles of what is right and wrong, not the fear of being different. Most important, this emotional nourishment helped them have the courage to stand up for their own principles.

Help children develop a resistance to negative peer pressure. Peer pressure is one of the most powerful forces in children's lives. By the time they are in their middle years, many children are increasingly more interested in belonging to their peer group than to their families. If you want to help your child establish and hang on to his own limits even amidst the pull of negative peer pressure, it is important to teach him how to evaluate what is being suggested by peers in order for him to make appropriate personal decisions that are consistent with "who he is" — his own strong ethic of behaving appropriately. To help your children learn decision-making, give them many daily choices, when appropriate, that help them see how to abide by their own positive self-image. With decision-making as a foundation, children are more able to muster the courage to stand by the decisions they make.

Teachable Moment

When Jamie got into trouble with a neighbor boy for throwing rocks at some other children, his answer to his mother's query about why he had done that was to say, "Josh said to do it."

"If he asked you to jump off a cliff, would you do that, too?" Denise asked in classic parent style.

"But if I don't do it, he won't be my friend," Jamie answered in his own defense.

It was then that Denise realized that she had not taught Jamie to withstand peer pressure. Part of the problem involved her sometimes authoritarian approach to her children. She thought that she should tell them what to do without offering choices. What she had inadvertently done was to teach her children to take orders.

"When somebody wants you to do something, how will you know whether or not to do it?" Denise asked Jamie.

"I guess I'd listen to that little voice inside me," Jamie answered.

"What little voice?" Denise pursued, a little worried that her youngest son was hearing voices.

"You know, my conscience," Jamie answered impatiently.

"Oh yes, your conscience." Denise was relieved. "And how will you know it's leading you in the right direction?"

"I don't know," Jamie answered after some thought.

"Well, I guess if you have to think about whether or not to do something, it's probably not a good idea to do it. That's your conscience telling you this information."

"But what if Josh wants to do something, and I know it's wrong and he keeps wanting me to do it?" Jamie asked helplessly.

"How about telling him that you like playing with him, but what he wants to do will get you both into trouble, and then suggest doing something else that you know is okay? Maybe we should practice a couple of times so you'll feel comfortable answering Josh."

Denise practiced with him, asking him to do all sorts of things, some of which he really had to think about because he wasn't sure if they were okay or not. Over the next few weeks, Jamie appeared to make better decisions about a lot of things. Denise felt really good when Jamie announced, "Josh asked me to go with him into the new house they're building over on the next block, but I thought about it and told him that we might get into trouble. Instead, we went over to the park and climbed on the playground stuff there. It was fun."

She knew that Jamie at least had the skills today that he needed to withstand peer pressure. She could only hope that he was courageous enough to continue to use them.

"Behold the turtle. He makes progress only when he sticks his neck out." — JAMES B. CONANT

7

HUMOR

"Humanity takes itself too seriously. It is the world's original sin. If the cavemen had known how to laugh, history would have been different."
— OSCAR WILDE

hu·mor *n* **1.** a comic quality causing amusement. *the humor of a situation* **2.** the faculty of perceiving, appreciating, or expressing what is amusing or comical **3.** comical writing or talk in general **4.** mental disposition or temperament **5.** a temporary mood or frame of mind: *He's in a bad humor today* **6.** a capricious or freakish inclination; whim or caprice; odd trait

- "That's funny. That makes me laugh."
- "Look at it this way. Then it's funny."
- "I feel so good when I laugh."
- "I like him because he makes me laugh."

HUMOR EVOKES A UNIQUELY human emotional response. Babies are able to laugh with joy at moments of discovery, simply bubbling over with the surprise of their growing awareness. But children can lose the virtue of humor when they feel unloved and when their lives lack models of how to flavor life with a sense of humor. To be able to see the humor in life requires an appreciation of its spontaneity and its imperfections. This appreciation is best developed in the context of a caring and supportive environment that encourages feeling a joyful sense of wonder about the world and looking for humor and solutions in adversity rather than looking for someone else to blame or to be responsible for life's ups and downs.

Humor is also used by children and adults as a defense against those situations that create anxiety. Intelligence, sex, religion, politics, and embarrassing situations all represent potentially stressful situations around which jokes are built in order to help us cope with our discomfort.

What Do We Mean by Humor?

- To find humor in life, a person must not take life too seriously.
- To have a sense of humor involves believing in oneself.
- Humor requires a creative view of our imperfect world.
- Accepting life as it is, is an element of humor.

Meet the Lewis Family

Bud and Karen Lewis loved their children, eight-year-old Kay, ten-year-old Brett, and thirteen-year-old Jason, but they tended to want perfection in a lot of things they demanded of the children. One day when Karen was ranting about how chores weren't being done the way she wanted, Jason told her to lighten up. Well, that was the last straw! She reacted by telling him how disrespectful he was and how ashamed she was that he was her son. Both statements tore at his heart. In retelling her encounter to Bud, Karen embellished the story until Jason was about to become number one on the 10 Most

Wanted list. It was then that Bud suggested that their family had somehow so covered up all the joy of their lives that it was now hard for him to come home at night. The whole family agreed to try to recapture the lost humor to rescue themselves from the quicksand of doom and gloom in which they were quickly sinking.

"If you laugh about mistakes, they don't bother you as much." — SAM

Teaching Tools

Model humor. The most important teaching tool parents possess is their ability to show children how to do things. Children want nothing more than to follow the example of those they love the most, so it is important that the example set is constructive. With humor, parents can show children how to find the fun in everyday life and how to accept the twists and turns that life has to offer.

WARNING: AVOID LAUGHING AT CHILDREN.

To show children humor, it is tempting to laugh at their mistakes. They may consider this parental laughter a put-down and lose their self-respect. Rather than laughing at children over something they did wrong, first ask them what they think about their mistake and then help them see the humor in what happened.

Teachable Moment

"Kay, would you please help me set the table?" Karen asked her daughter before dinner.

"Okay, Mommy," she answered, and she opened the cabinet where the drinking glasses were kept. As she began taking a glass out for each member of the family, she dropped one on the kitchen floor and it broke.

"Oh noooooo!" she cried, and she ran out of the kitchen sobbing.

Karen went after her. "Kay, honey, what's wrong?" she asked.

"I broke a glass," the eight-year-old wailed. "I'm so clumsy."

"Everybody makes mistakes, sweetheart," Karen told her. "Breaking a glass is no big deal. What's a big deal is breaking all the glasses. Or worse yet, breaking all the dishes. Then we'd have to hold our food in our hands and lap up our drinks like dogs do."

As Kay pictured what her mother described, she began to giggle. She could imagine her family eating like a family of dogs, and it really struck her as funny. She and her mother then went into the kitchen to clean the broken glass up from the floor. Karen was pleased with herself that she was able to see humor in the face of adversity and that humor neutralized the disaster that Kay believed she had caused.

"When you can see the funny side, it's a lot easier."
— Katie

Reinforce humor in children. Parents are often in a dilemma about how to react when their children say things that strike the parents as funny. Why? Because other people might not find them as humorous, depending on how they define "offensive." Therefore, in order to reinforce humor, you must first make a judgment as to whether or not it is appropriate. One definition of appropriate humor is that which avoids cruelty to others or putting them down. You might also wish to discourage humor that involves bodily functions or sex. Simply reacting as an appreciative audience is sufficient reinforcement for most budding comics. It is also helpful to understand the developmental nature of humor in children. Young children up to about age six enjoy humor about the process of elimination, so humor may focus on "poop" and similar words. For six-to-twelve-year-olds, more sophisticated elimination and bodily function words may be used, and underwear may be a popular focus of humor. Teenage humor may take on a more sexual content involving more graphic expressions.

WARNING: AVOID OVERREACTING TO SCATOLOGICAL HUMOR.

Because children naturally use humor to reduce their anxiety about the things that are happening to them, overreacting to any offensive use of humor will only increase their anxiety and help them feel ashamed of themselves. When they're anxious and ashamed, children might still behave inappropriately, but that behavior will go underground and parents may no longer be aware that it's still being bandied about.

Teachable Moment

Karen and Bud took their children to a band concert in the park one Sunday afternoon in an attempt to let them see a "real" band rather than a band on TV. One of the numbers involved two men playing bagpipes.

"What do they have in those bags? Cats?" Brett asked with mock seriousness.

Taken by surprise, both Karen and Bud began to laugh, as did several people who were sitting nearby. "Brett, that's funny!" Karen said, and Brett beamed with her approval.

By reinforcing Brett's appropriate humor, Karen was able to allow him to take a creative and humorous view of a new experience that could have made him feel dumb because he was unfamiliar with it.

"I like anybody that's funny." — BRAD

Monitor television and movies. Because children are just becoming familiar with what is considered funny, they might learn inappropriate humor that is hurtful to others by what they see in the media. When someone in a situation comedy makes a derogatory comment about another person, and the audience or laugh track laughs, children become conditioned to think that what was said was funny. In order to help your children understand the inappropriateness of some of the attempts at humor they are seeing, watch what they are watching and help them understand that appropriate humor doesn't involve hurting others.

Teachable Moment

Being concerned about what her children were watching, Karen decided to spend some time watching Kay and Brett's favorite programs with them. One of the programs was a situation comedy involving children. When one of the boys called the other a "butt-head," the TV audience laughed, and Karen's children laughed right along with them.

"What's so funny about calling someone a butt-head?" Karen asked.

"Mom, it's just so funny," Kay answered

"Butt-head . . . Butt-head!" Brett kept saying.

"How would you feel if I called you a butt-head?" Karen asked her son, who suddenly became sober.

"I don't think I'd like it much," he finally answered.

"I wouldn't like it either," Kay agreed.

"I guess we need to think about how the person feels who is being called a bad name, even if it is supposed to be funny," Karen continued. "To know if it's okay to say something like that, just think how you'd feel if somebody said that to you."

Later that week while watching TV with a friend, Karen overheard Brett say, "That's not really funny. That'd hurt someone's feelings if we said it to them."

"Who cares?" the friend responded. "It's funny."

"Well, I care, and I don't want to hurt people's feelings," Brett answered.

Karen was pleased that her son was able to use some discretion in evaluating the difference between humor that was "right" and "wrong" to use.

Let people know when their humor hurts. Sometimes attempts to be funny are hurtful to others, leading to the old saying "Many a truth were told in jest." But because it was said in a humorous way, this kind of joking is supposed to be okay. Sarcasm and put-downs are often ways that humor is used to damage people's self-esteem, as a way of one-upmanship. In order for children to learn the hurtful nature of some humor, boundaries should be put around their use of humor, and children should be taught just how it feels to be on the receiving end of some sarcastic passes even when thrown in for "fun."

WARNING: AVOID FIGHTING FIRE WITH FIRE.

When children are being sarcastic or violating other humor boundaries, it is tempting to use the same kind of humor in retaliation. The use of sarcasm to combat sarcasm only models the kind of humor violations you are trying to eliminate. It is best to inform the comedian of the hurt experienced and suggest other ways for him to express his feelings or ideas.

Teachable Moment

"Jason, we've all decided to go to the movies together this Friday night," Karen told her teenager, "so don't make any other plans."

"Right, Mom!" Jason responded sarcastically. "I'm going to miss being with my friends to watch a geeky G-rated movie with my family. Get a life! You are such a dweeb."

Karen's emotions said, "Rip his tongue out!" but her voice of reason said, "Jason, that really hurts my feelings when you call me names and are sarcastic about our family plans."

"Can't you take a joke, Mom?" Jason said defensively. "I was only kidding."

"I understand that you were trying to be funny, but your attempt at humor was hurtful and not appropriate," Karen responded. "In order to keep your privileges, you'll have to keep your humor in check. No more hurtful sarcasm or name-calling will be allowed. If you have to tell somebody that you were just kidding, then what you've said to them is too hurtful. Understand?"

"Gee, Mom!" Jason responded. "Don't be so serious. I don't think it's that big of a deal."

"Well, it's a big deal to the person whose feelings you've hurt," Karen reasoned. "All I'm asking is that you listen to yourself before you say anything and try to imagine how the other person might feel. That way maybe you'll know if you're being hurtful or not. Think before you speak. Sometimes it's not what you say but how you say it that can hurt someone's feelings. Your privileges depend on your learning this lesson."

"Okay, Mom, I'll try. But you know me — anything for a laugh."

In spite of his being a teen, Karen knew Jason would follow her restrictions. He was sensitive to others and did care about their feelings. He just needed to learn how to push the stop button on his sense of humor, something she was glad to be teaching him.

"A person has two legs and one sense of humor, and if you're faced with the choice, it's better to lose a leg." — CHARLES LINDER

8

RESPECT

"True politeness is perfect ease in freedom. It simply consists in treating others just as you love to be treated yourself." — EARL OF CHESTERFIELD

> **re·spect** *vb.* to consider worthy of high regard: ESTEEM *n.* **1.** the quality or state of being esteemed: HONOR **2.** expressions of respect or deference

- "I'm sorry I offended you. I didn't think about how you might feel."

- "When I go out to eat, I'm so glad that my little sister doesn't make a lot of noise."

- "I didn't do that because I knew it was against the rules."

- "I wanted something from your room but I didn't go in it. I didn't want to invade your privacy."

IT'S A VICIOUS CYCLE. To be able to respect others and the limits they set, one must be blessed with a sense of respect for oneself. How is that blessing attained? By being treated with respect! Therefore, in teaching children respect, parents have the responsibility to understand their child's viewpoint in different situations and be respectful of those positions, even if they don't agree with them. Through the modeling of understanding and acceptance of others, a child will also learn to try to understand others. By being able to think from another person's perspective — even if it's different from their own — children will learn to treat others with kindness and caring. When they do, children will learn this lesson: Respect is reciprocal. People are much more likely to attain success in personal relationships and in professional goals when they respect the people with whom they work and play. What a treat it is when children do learn to respect limits and have internalized boundaries that guide behavior! These "wonderful children," as neighbors label them, can then spend their time developing strong character — not developing alibis for the trouble they have brewed.

"J think it is important to establish and respect limits, because then you won't dig yourself a hole you can't get out of." — JULIE

WHAT DO WE MEAN BY RESPECT?

- Respect means caring about the rights of others, even if they infringe upon one's own rights.
- When thinking about another person in a positive way, one shows respect for that person.
- By caring about the feelings of others, a person shows respect for himself, too. He is treating others the way he wants to be treated.
- Admiring another person or a person's traits is a way of showing respect.
- When a person has good self-esteem, he demonstrates that he also respects himself.

MEET THE SAMUELS FAMILY

Clarence and Laveeta Samuels realized that their thirteen-year-old daughter, Tonya, and seven-year-old twin daughters, Ella and Etta, thought nothing of their behavior when they talked back to their parents, took clothing from each other without asking, and nonchalantly called each other nasty names. The couple was so upset about their rude and insensitive actions that they, too, became rude and insensitive, calling them "stupid" and "crazy" and then sending them to their rooms without dinner on occasion. As their anger multiplied, their children's antics did, too. The girls didn't become any more respectful; in fact, they seemed to have less respect for their parents and for each other than ever before. Clarence and Laveeta knew they were fighting a losing battle. They decided that they must change their respect refrain if they wanted their girls to dance to more thoughtful tunes around their family, friends, and community.

TEACHING TOOLS

Treat children with respect. "Children are people, too!" you may have heard someone say. Taking that statement to heart is the beginning step in teaching respect to children. If you set out each day to treat your children as if they were guests in your home, you will show them by example that you hold them in esteem. That's not to say that you should forgo the rules, however. Children need rules and should be accountable for following them, but you can deliver consequences for rule violations in a respectful way. Try to remember what it felt like to be their ages—four, eight, ten, or a teenager—as a first step to realizing that the definition of a problem is "something that is of concern to me," even if it seems trivial to another person.

WARNING: DON'T ATTACK YOUR CHILD'S CHARACTER.

When parents become angry with children, it's easy to focus on what appears to be the child's character rather than to deal with the behavior in question. Such statements as "Don't be stupid!" and "Don't be a crybaby!" are but two examples of character assassination. To avoid attacking character, think about the behavior of the child and how that behavior might change. Behavior change ultimately leads to a change in character.

Teachable Moment

When Laveeta Samuels gave her girls some juice one morning, some if it was spilled when Ella and Etta were passing the muffins. In the past, Laveeta had yelled at them for being so clumsy, but this time she thought about how the same situation might be handled if she were serving a friend or neighbor and that person accidentally spilled something. She certainly wouldn't yell and tell them they were clumsy! She would simply clean it up and get a replacement.

"I'm sorry the juice was spilled," she then said to her daughters. "Now we have to clean it up. Etta, you can get the sponge by the sink; and Ella, you get some paper towels. We'll have this cleaned up in a minute."

Not only did the girls feel better about the whole incident, but so did Laveeta. She saw proof of the way that being considerate of her girls' feelings improved their cooperation and each of their relationships. She remembered how it felt to spill things accidentally . . . and was glad that her parents didn't make her feel like a loser when she made a mistake. That was a lesson worth passing on to her children.

Teach children to understand the position of others.   In order to have respect for another person, one must be able to understand life from that person's point of view. To teach your children to think about another's viewpoint or role, it is important to ask them to put themselves in the other person's shoes.

Teachable Moment

At bedtime one evening, Etta began to talk about a problem she was having with a friend at school. Clarence and Laveeta knew it was late, and they were both tired and wanted some time alone; but they also knew that Etta's problem was important and real to her. "I'm so sorry that you and Shelly aren't getting along right now. Is there anything you can think of that might fix this problem?" they asked.

They then proceeded to help Etta do some problem-solving by helping her explore her options and look at potential outcomes of each option. Etta was then able to go to sleep satisfied that she had some ideas to try the next day that might help her best friend and her stay best friends.

Praise kind and caring acts.   In order to encourage others to respect you, it is important to learn to treat *them* with respect. Encourage this aspect of kindness in your children by suggesting caring things that they can do for each other. When you catch them in the act of doing good things for others, praise the behavior so that your children connect respect with your approval.

WARNING: DON'T LECTURE.

The lecture method of instruction is the least likely way to teach children about issues of respect. Lecture creates a situation in which children quickly lose interest, and as boredom sets in, they learn how not to listen. Rather than lecture, model what you want them to learn, and set rules and boundaries for their behavior.

Teachable Moment

"I think we need a new rule in our home," Laveeta said one day after the girls had been squabbling about who sat in the best chair for their favorite TV program. "Every day, you must do at least two kind acts for each other. Then you'll each see how good you feel inside when you are respectful of others."

Laveeta listened in silence to the loud protests her children gave her in return for her bright idea, and then Etta asked cautiously, "What if we don't do nice things for each other?"

"I'm glad you asked that, because I left out the good part," Laveeta answered. "We're going to use Grandma's Rule: When you've done what you have to do, then you get to do what you want to do. For this new rule, to get to do what you want to do tomorrow, you have to do two kind acts for each other today. If you choose not to do nice things for each other, then that means you have chosen to give up doing what you like tomorrow."

"That's not fair," the girls wailed in unison, one of the few cooperative things they had done for a while.

"I understand how you feel, but the rule stands," Laveeta calmly informed them. "Remember, starting today, you must do two kind things for each other in order to get to do what you want to do tomorrow. And so that I know that you've done kind things for each other, at the end of the day I'll ask each of you to tell me what the other has done for you."

Using Grandma's Rule (when you do *x*, then you can do *y*), which offers daily privileges as a reward for appropriate behavior, and asking each to report on the other reinforces the importance of this positive behavior and gives it more attention than the negative behavior. In addition, letting the children know the consequences of following (and breaking!) the rule lets them be in charge of their choices.

Later that day, Laveeta observed Ella asking Etta if she wanted anything from the kitchen because she was going to get a snack. "Asking Etta if she wanted a snack showed you respected her enough to want to do something for her. I'm sure it made her feel good that you cared enough to ask, and I'll bet it made you feel good, too," her mom noted. By describing the behavior when she praised it, Laveeta left no doubt about her expectations of respecting others, and gave it her coveted stamp of approval as well.

Model acts of respect. Adults can establish behaviors of respect by doing these simple respectful things not only for their children but also for each other: using good manners, asking permission of each other before you do things like switching the channel on the TV, allowing privacy, and simply listening to someone when he is talking. Once you are aware of the importance of being sensitive to others' needs, you will be surprised at how easy it is to choose to be respectful of those near and dear to your heart.

Teachable Moment

> When Clarence knew he was going to be late coming home from work, he always called. Laveeta then took the opportunity to point out to the girls that act of respect. "Your dad always lets me know if he's going to be late," she beamed, showing how much that meant to her. "Isn't that nice of him? He doesn't want us to worry." A simple comment is all that was needed from this mother to reinforce the respectful behavior that their father showed her.

Listen to your children. Examples of "listening" being an important skill have been part of popular culture since the first secret was told with the warning "Don't tell!" From songwriters to sex therapists, people know listening is crucial to building relationships you can trust. In fact, the best way to model respect is to listen to others. When your children talk, look them straight in the eyes and listen to what they have to say. Then restate what they said in your own words so that they know you heard them. Compliment any good ideas and constructive thoughts they have so that they know you are respecting what they have to say. If the thoughts don't make sense or are leading in a direction you would prefer they didn't take, either ignore the comments or restate them as you think they might have been meant. You are then providing a model for the way that your children might share what's on their minds today and in the future.

Teachable Moment

> Clarence was watching the ball game on television when Ella came to him and asked his advice about

her homework. "Daddy, can you help me with this problem?"

Clarence didn't want to do homework. He wanted to watch the game, and he could feel his irritation rise. "Wait a minute, Ella! Can't you see that I'm watching this game? Can't that wait?" he shouted. But when he saw the look of hurt and disappointment in her face, he shifted his thinking away from feeling sorry for himself and tried to put himself in his daughter's place. He understood that his reaction to her showed Ella that he didn't have much respect for her need for help.

"I'm sorry, sweetheart, I can help. Here, let me turn the sound off so we won't be distracted by the game. Now, what about this problem?" he asked, quickly changing his tune. They quickly finished the problem, too, and he went back to his game while Ella skipped happily off to do the rest of her homework — content with the attention and information the homework session had provided.

Later Etta was trying to explain something that had happened at school. "Then on the playground, Mindy actually ignored me as if I wasn't there," she lamented. "I hate her."

"You say she pretended that you weren't there so she didn't have to play with you, and you hate her for not playing with you?" Clarence asked, remembering the "Active Listening" workshop they had recently had at work.

"Well, no," Etta answered as she reflected on what Clarence had said. "I don't actually hate her for not playing with me. It was mean of her to ignore me, though, don't you think?"

"It would have been nice if she hadn't ignored you and

had told you that she wanted to play with someone else, but she didn't," Clarence answered. "How would you have treated Mindy if you had wanted to play with somebody else while she was around?"

"I don't know," Etta responded. "I guess I'd tell her, but I wouldn't want to hurt her feelings. I know I wouldn't just ignore her."

Their conversation shifted to other topics, and Clarence was pleased that he had been able to listen to both his girls that day and to help them think through problems that they were having. He knew the importance of being there for his girls even though it was hard for him to give time to them.

Respect children's privacy. So that children can understand what the term "privacy" means, it is important for parents to allow them their own privacy and to respect it. Such simple acts as knocking and asking permission to enter before going into a child's room convey the feeling that you do have respect for his possessions and space — and his needs for these to be separate from everyone else's in the family.

WARNING: DON'T VIOLATE PRIVATE SPACE.

As hard as it is to let your children's "secrets" be just that, violations of their private space such as snooping in rooms, listening in on telephone conversations, reading notes to and from friends, and entering before knocking all violate privacy and trust. In the face of such violations, it is impossible for children to trust adults and to learn that respecting privacy is a valuable lesson.

Teachable Moment

When Tonya turned thirteen, it seemed as though she suddenly became distant and secretive. Laveeta missed the confidences that her daughter had always shared with her and was afraid that her teenager was doing something she shouldn't; but she didn't know how to find out what she was really up to. Then one day, the opportunity to do so fell right in her lap. She found one of Tonya's many notes that she and her friends were constantly exchanging lying right smack in front of her on the floor next to the laundry basket. Laveeta froze; she knew she should just let it be, leave it lying on the floor where it was rather than to devour it the way she wanted.

Finally, her curiosity got the better of her. She picked up the note, opened it, and read it. Laveeta was appalled by the language Tonya's friend used in the note, but to her great relief, there was really nothing in the note that concerned her. Her feelings of peace were shattered the next moment, however, when Tonya burst into her room and caught her in the act of espionage.

"Mom! Were you reading that note?" Tonya screamed. "How could you?"

"Tonya, I'm really sorry," her mother babbled. "I know I shouldn't have. It was an invasion of your privacy. Please forgive me. I won't do it again, I promise."

This "first offense" on her mom's part taught both family members a valuable lesson: Respecting another's privacy is an important part of keeping a relationship between two people healthy and trusting.

Model respect for privacy in your own life. When adults show children that they respect each other's possessions and private time, their children then have a concrete model to follow when they are asked to respect the boundaries of others.

Teachable Moment

Clarence and Laveeta always respected each other's need for his or her own space. They never opened each other's mail, refrained from asking who was on the phone when a conversation ended, and they always asked permission to use each other's possessions. Because it wasn't clear to them that their children had a clue about respect for other people's boundaries, even though *they* did, Clarence and Laveeta decided to call their respectful behaviors (which they had previously taken for granted) to their children's attention.

"Mmmm. A package for your mother. I wonder what's in it," Clarence said to the children as he put the mail on the counter in the kitchen.

"Here, let me open it!" Ella shouted eagerly. "I want to know what it is!"

"No, we can't open it. The package belongs to your mother, and it wouldn't be right to invade your mother's privacy like that," Clarence explained.

"Why not?" Tonya joined the discussion. "We're all in the same family. What's hers is ours, isn't it?"

"Yes, we are in the same family, but that's not the point. Even though we all live together, we should respect each other's privacy," her dad explained. "How would you feel if we opened your mail? It's the same thing, you know."

"Yeah, I guess," Etta answered. "But I still want to know what's in the package."

"If your mom wants you to know, she'll tell you,"

Clarence concluded the lesson, giving the responsibility for giving up privacy to its rightful owner.

Allow children to have time alone. Children often need to be alone for periods of time as they reflect upon experiences, deal with those that are confusing or upsetting, or just to bounce a ball or play with their favorite toys or collector's items. This is especially true of children entering into and those already in adolescence. Creating "alone time" when children are young helps them understand the need for spending some time entertaining themselves and teaches them that parents need time to themselves, too. For young children, rest time that eventually replaces nap time can be the beginning of their having specific time alone. Helping children create interesting activities during their alone time makes that time seem less boring and useless.

Teachable Moment

When Ella and Etta were four years old, Laveeta decided to continue their daily nap time even after the children outgrew the need for a nap. She changed the nap time to "quiet time" and encouraged independent activities during this quiet time, even when the children wanted to be entertained.

"I want to watch TV!" Ella demanded one day when her mother told her and Etta that it was quiet time.

"I'm sorry," her mother stated matter-of-factly, "I know you would rather be entertained, but you can find something fun to do. And when you have entertained yourself for an hour, then you may watch TV, go out to play, or help me make some cookies. I need some quiet time, and I think you and Etta do, too. I'll see you in an hour."

The habit of quiet time continued on the weekends as

the children became busier with their after-school activities. Laveeta also liked the time for herself, for it allowed her to think about her day or the evening ahead, and, in some cases, to get some cooking done without interruptions. She did value her privacy and felt more satisfied and happier when she knew it was valued by her family, too.

Encourage private space. Children need to have private space that they can call their own. This private space may be as small as a shoe box filled with those things considered special, or as large as a tree house or playroom. By adolescence, a child's own room may become that most private of sanctuaries. By allowing your children's private space, you are teaching them that privacy is special and deserves to be respected.

Teachable Moment

Etta was a collector of everything that she thought was important, whether anyone else thought so or not! She kept her collections in a group of shoe boxes on a shelf in her closet. Tonya thought her collections were stupid "baby" things, and she often made fun of them — much to her parents' dismay.

One day after Etta had been particularly annoying to her, Tonya went into Etta's room and emptied her shoe boxes into her wastebasket. "It's just trash, you know," she sneered when Etta discovered what her older sister had done.

When Etta told their dad about it, he took Tonya aside to explain to her the damage she had done. "How would you feel if Etta had gone into your room and dumped all your makeup in the trash, or read your diary or notes from your friends?"

"That little creep!" she squealed. "She'd better not ever do that. I'd kill her."

Without any more conversation, Tonya understood that she should not do something to her sister that she would not appreciate being done to her.

"Okay, Dad, I'm sorry. I'll go apologize to her. I understand how she feels."

"I'm sure she'll appreciate your apology, Tonya," her dad said. "Now, because we have rules about privacy here, you'll have to make up for violating hers. You must do Etta's chores for one week, and I hope you consider privacy more carefully from now on."

By helping Tonya understand her sister's feelings and giving her a way to make up to her sister for what she had done, Clarence not only reinforced the need to respect another's privacy but taught her the lesson that when privacy is violated, there is a price to pay.

"There is a certain limit with everyone; once you pass over it, you may have a hard time coming back."
— SHAUNA

Let privacy rules root children. In order to fully illustrate the need for people to respect each other, parents must develop and maintain rules to follow in order to know where boundaries stop and start. Such rules as "Knock Before Entering" and "Ask Before Borrowing" are important boundary rules. Enforcement of such rules involves posting them for all family members to see, praising children's behavior when they follow the rules, and using negative consequences when rules are violated.

WARNING: DON'T USE STRONG PUNISHMENT FOR VIOLATIONS OF PRIVACY.

When children violate privacy, strong punishment will only create anger and a loss of respect for the adult delivering the punishment. When children lose respect for adults, they are less likely to want to follow the rules and code of behavior parents are trying to teach.

Teachable Moment

"Ella's been spying on me when I'm changing my clothes," Tonya screeched at her mother. "Make the little creep stop!"

"Ella shouldn't be invading your privacy like that. I'll talk to her," her mom comforted. She went to Ella's room and knocked on the door. When Ella gave permission for her to come in, Laveeta talked to her about her invasion of Tonya's privacy.

"Tonya is upset because you've been sneaking into her room to spy on her when she's getting dressed," her mother began calmly. "I understand your curiosity, but you're invading her privacy. You know how upset you have gotten when she has seen you in your underwear. Well, that's how she feels. Please have respect for your sister's right to privacy."

Laveeta explained the family rule to Ella once again — we respect each other's privacy — and reminded her that part of that respect meant staying out of each other's room when the door is closed.

"Now, because you violated her privacy, you have to make it up to her by doing her chores for the rest of the week," Laveeta continued. "After that, I hope you will have as much respect for her privacy as you want for your own."

Set and enforce rules. At the core of learning to respect others is the ability to internalize and use rules. Unfortunately, children don't come into the world with their own built-in set of rules, so their parents must be the first rule-setting agents. To set rules for your children, state rules about what you want your children to be doing. These "do" rules put goals of appropriate behavior before your children. Once the rules are set, let the rules stand by themselves, making them an emotionless focus of your children's attack. If *you* become the rule, then your children will see you as the one to test. Enforcing the rules simply involves making the following of rules the key to all privileges.

WARNING: DON'T USE SEVERE PUNISHMENT FOR RULE VIO-LATIONS.

When children fail to follow rules, parents often think that they will make them atone for their inappropriate behavior by giving them harsh punishment. However, this plan almost always backfires. Instead of helping them remember the rules, severe punishment makes children resentful and leads them to thinking about revenge instead of thinking about rules and how to follow them. In order to help children behave within limits, reinforce the following of the rules of your household and let the natural consequences of not doing so, such as losing privileges, act as reminders.

Teachable Moment

Clarence and Laveeta decided that there should be some basic house rules to govern the behavior of their children at home. One most important rule involved the constant fighting between the children. Ella seemed to want to dominate her sister and often demanded that Etta move when Ella wanted to sit in the chair Etta always sat in at the dinner table. Ella also demanded total control of what television programs they watched. Etta was so used to Ella's abuse that she would fight back without thinking that she might be hurting her sister.

"We have a new rule," Laveeta announced to the children. "The rule is that you have to get along with each other. When you are getting along, then you get to do what you want to do within our new house rules. If you choose not to get along, then you will have to go to time-out. Do you understand?"

"You mean if dumb Etta doesn't do what I want, then I go to time-out?" Ella asked. (For the definition of time-out, please turn to page 50.)

"All you have to do is get along with each other. If you choose not to for any reason, then you *both* have to go to time-out. That's the rule!" Laveeta answered, ignoring Ella's name-calling in order to focus on the rule to be enforced.

As the day progressed, Laveeta made it a point to keep reminding her children of the "getting along" rule by praising the fact that they were respecting each other. "You are getting along so nicely," she would say when she saw them swinging in the backyard. But later the inevitable happened. Etta came running to her mother claiming that Ella hit her when she wouldn't give up the television remote.

"I'm so sorry you both have chosen not to get along. Ella, I want you to go to time-out right here. Etta, I want you to sit in the other room — the kitchen," Laveeta said.

"But I . . ." Ella began, but Laveeta cut her short.

"Ella, the rule was to get along," Laveeta said calmly, "and you chose not to do that. You knew the rule. Now you have to go to time-out."

The children grudgingly did time in isolation, and over

the next several weeks, Clarence and Laveeta noticed that the fighting between the girls faded to nothing. The positive rewards of getting to do what they wanted when they got along was the motivation they needed to respect the home-base behavior limits.

Reinforce respect for rule-following. When children do follow rules, it is important to call it to their attention through warm, caring, verbal praise. When you praise your children's behavior, they will focus on the positive rewards from doing whatever won the praise, and want to do it again.

WARNING: DON'T USE TANGIBLE REWARDS.

Children who are rewarded with stickers, candy, toys, and other tangible items for following rules or for conforming to limits will grow to believe that they must be paid something for their appropriate behavior. The behavior rules children follow need to be internalized and rewarded by the good feelings inside.

Teachable Moment

Laveeta was gratified when she saw that Etta had remembered to make her bed before she came to breakfast. Doing so was a new rule for the children, and Laveeta wasn't sure that it would be followed.

"Etta, you made your bed this morning. That was so thoughtful of you. That will help me because I won't have to do it, and I can do other things instead. Thank you so much for remembering the rule," Laveeta said.

Later that week, she noticed that Tonya was also making her bed regularly, something she honestly didn't expect her to do. Tonya had overheard the praise that her mom had given Etta and wanted to get in on the attention. "Tonya, you are showing such responsibility in following the rule about making your bed," Laveeta noted. "That helps me so much. Thank you!"

Teach children about the feelings of others. In order to understand the need for internal limits and to develop good manners, children must be able to think about the feelings of others. To help children learn how their behavior might impact those feelings, it is important to point out how others might feel when they behave in certain ways. To teach your children how others feel, talk to them about the impact they make on you and on other people.

Teachable Moment

Laveeta and her children were in a shopping center when they noticed an old man having problems getting onto the escalator. Ella laughed and said, "Look at that old guy! He can't walk!"

"Ella, that was a very unkind thing to say," Laveeta told her. "How do you suppose he would feel if he heard you say that? What if that were your grandfather? Would you like for people to be saying things like that about him?"

"Well, it's not," Ella answered gruffly. "He couldn't hear what I was saying, Mommy!"

"Let's make a new rule," Laveeta answered matter-of-factly. "Before we say anything, let's think about how the other person might feel if we said it, even if we don't think that person can hear it. That way, we can stop ourselves from saying something that might hurt someone's feelings."

Reinforce good manners. Manners are simply skills designed to help make other people feel comfortable. They help with social interaction by offering guidelines and limits to social behavior. In order for your children to understand and respect the social limits provided by manners, they need to know what the limits are and the impact that bad manners might have on people.

Teachable Moment

At dinner, Ella had a bad habit of belching loudly. She thought it was a very funny thing to do, and that belief was sometimes reinforced by her sisters, her dad, or one of her friends, who would laugh when it happened. Then one day Ella came home from a friend's house and asked her mother why her friend's mother had told her that it was bad manners to belch at the table.

"We were eating lunch, and I belched. Mrs. Thompson said that it was bad manners and that I couldn't do that when I was eating at Erin's house." Obviously, Ella was confused about the discrepancy in rules.

Clarence and Laveeta decided that they had been too lenient in setting limits for their children and that it was time to teach them appropriate table manners before their friends' parents would forbid them to eat at their homes. They started with dinnertime rules which were based on manners.

"Here are the new dinner rules," Clarence announced. "When we practice these, we will feel good about our behavior, and others will be glad to be in our company. These are rules that ladies and gentlemen all over the world use. First, we must all sit up straight at the dinner table. Then we have to remember to chew with our mouths closed. When we want to talk, we have to have our mouths empty. We have to keep our left hand in our laps with our napkins, and no loud belching at the table."

"What if we don't do that?" Etta asked, wanting to know the boundaries around these new rules. There were so many! she thought.

"Those who can follow the new manners rules will get to stay at the table and eat with the family. Those who can't will have to eat by themselves in the kitchen," Laveeta answered. "And we're going to make this a contest to see who can follow the most rules at the table. Here's a list of the rules to remind you so you don't forget. We'll read them every night until we know them by heart."

"When we can all follow the manners rules for two weeks, then we can go out to eat. I know how much you like to do that," Clarence added.

Manners dramatically improved in the Samuels household, without whining, nagging behavior from "rule-setters." The rules were established and *they* set the behavior pace. The role that Clarence and Laveeta played was the "praise doctors," reinforcing their children each day for following the manners rules.

"You cannot shake hands with a clenched fist."
— INDIRA GANDHI

9

LOYALTY

"A friend is a present you give yourself." — ROBERT
LOUIS STEVENSON

loy·al *adj.* **1.** faithful to one's allegiance, as to a sovereign, government, or state: *a loyal subject* **2.** faithful to one's oath, commitments, or obligations: *to be loyal to a vow* **3.** faithful to any person or thing conceived of as deserving fidelity or imposing obligations: *a loyal friend*

∘ "But, Mom! He's my friend and he needs my help."

∘ "Yes, I will, Daddy. I promised."

∘ "I made a commitment to have this done, and I'm going to get it done."

∘ "Today is spirit day at school, and I want to wear the school colors."

∘ "Yes, I know I'm not supposed to fight, but I couldn't let them do that to my brother."

"BE TRUE TO YOUR school, just like you're true to your girl," the Beach Boys wrote in a 1960s song. These images in this song are healthy and heartwarming because they evoke a sense of attachment, of meaning, of belonging. People need to feel connected to their surroundings — be they fellow human beings, their workplace, their preschool, or their pets! This rule of human behavior is a powerful one. If we feel good about the things we are attached to, then we feel good about ourselves because of those attachments.

Lessons in loyalty begin with the first secure attachment an infant makes with a caring adult and are reinforced through those who create a sense of family for the child. But learning to be loyal to one's family is only the introduction to these lessons. Expanding the definition of loyalty learned in the family to include those things and people one cares about in the community — the poor, the hungry, the homeless, the less fortunate — involves being willing to make sacrifices for others, because you care so much. Underlying these caring feelings is the ability to make a commitment to the greater good of mankind, remembering all the while that loyalty begins at home.

WHAT DO WE MEAN BY LOYALTY?

° A loyal person keeps the promises he makes.
° Loyalty involves learning to care about people enough to keep our commitments to them.
° In some cases, loyalty means making sacrifices for the benefit of others.
° Loyalty involves allegiance to a cause.

MEET THE MCCOY-PORTER FAMILY

Both Dave and Britt McCoy-Porter, parents of six-year-old George McCoy and ten-year-old Debbie McCoy, worked outside their home. Their children loved their neighborhood elementary school, where Britt was active in the PTA and Dave was in the Dads and Daughters Club. One day,

Debbie told her family at dinner that children had been vandalizing the school and the neighborhood.

"They aren't being very loyal to their school, are they?" Dave commented.

"Or the neighborhood," Britt added. "If they cared about where they lived and went to school, these children wouldn't be messing them up."

"What do you mean?" curious George asked. George was hungry for information about everything, and his parents were delighted to feed him answers, particularly answers about important virtues like loyalty.

"Cherish others' property." — JESSICA

TEACHING TOOLS

Model loyalty. To help children understand how to be loyal, examples of loyal behavior must be pointed out to them as often as possible. Keeping promises and commitments and participating in chores that help keep the family organized and "working" are ways of role-modeling being loyal to people. Wearing school colors on school spirit day and observing national holidays are two subtler ways to transmit messages about "loyalty to institutions" to the next generation.

WARNING: AVOID SHOWING DISLOYALTY.

Children who are being encouraged to show loyalty to friends and institutions will have difficulty understanding the dual standard if they see their parents criticizing those very people and places. Talking about relatives, former spouses, and family friends in negative ways shows a level of disloyalty, and being openly critical of teachers and other authority figures to whom your children are loyal will only undermine the lessons you want them to learn.

Teachable Moment

"I promised to go over to Hank's today to help him put new brakes in his car," Dave told Britt at breakfast on Saturday morning.

"But we wanted you here with us today," Debbie complained, overhearing the conversation. "Now we won't see you all day."

"Yes, I know, sweetheart," Dave answered. "But I promised my friend I'd help. After all, he is my friend, and I think I need to be loyal to him when he needs something."

"Your dad's right," Britt agreed. "We can have your dad all day tomorrow. He needs to help his friend today."

Reinforce family commitment. Children who feel strongly connected to their family are learning about family loyalty by putting family needs above their own. A major way to help children connect to the family is to establish family duties. In order to help your children establish and maintain strong family connections, make chore lists for each child and insist that the chores be completed. Tell your children how important their efforts are to the welfare of the family so that they gain a sense of being needed.

WARNING: AVOID PUNISHING CHILDREN FOR FAILING TO DO CHORES.

Children who are punished don't learn loyalty to their families, because the punishment makes them feel anger and resentment. Rather than using punishment, use Grandma's Rule, which demands that children do what they are required to do before they get to do what they want to do. By forgoing privileges until chores are done, children are not only free to establish family loyalty, but they also learn not to procrastinate.

Teachable Moment

When Britt noticed that George and Debbie were not doing their chores every day, she decided this might be a good time to talk about family loyalty.

"I really need your help to keep our family going," Britt said. "When you neglect your chores, I have to do them. For our family to be able to have time to play, we all have to work together and help each other. We owe it to each other to help."

"But we don't like to do all that work," George said honestly. "It's no fun to work all the time."

"I understand how you feel," Britt responded. "But I do need your help. I'll tell you what. When your chores are done every day, then you will get to do what you like to do."

"Do you mean we can't watch TV or play with our friends or anything until we get our chores done?" Debbie asked. "That's not fair!"

"Well, is it fair that you are a part of this family and yet you don't have to do anything to help the family?" Britt answered. "I don't think that's a very efficient family system for us to use."

The children grumbled, but the chores were done every day, and Britt was lavish in her praise for their cooperation. "Thank you so much for the help you're giving our family. You are showing such loyalty!" she told them.

By presenting the need to help the family as the motivating reason to do chores, George and Debbie understood that their doing their chores was an important part of family life — not just a waste of time, as they had previously thought.

"My parents made up this thing where our family is on a 'team,' and whenever someone on our team is in trouble, we get off the bench to help them." —KATIE

Teach children to be loyal to others as well as to themselves. In order for children to continue to develop the behaviors that reflect loyalty, they need to receive positive feedback when they show loyalty. Good praise involves a description of the specific behavior and a connection between that behavior and the concept you are trying to teach.

Teachable Moment

Whenever Britt or Dave saw the children doing something that reflected loyalty, they didn't hesitate to point it out. One day when Debbie had a playmate, Sally, over, Sally said, "Your brother is such a geek! How can you stand him?"

Debbie answered this put-down by saying, "He's my brother, and we're a family. If you don't like him, that's your problem."

When Sally left, Dave said, "Debbie, I heard you stand up for your brother today. I was so happy to hear your family loyalty!"

"If you cannot be loyal to yourself, you cannot learn to be loyal to others." — TANNER

Help children assume the role of others. When children put themselves in the position of another person, they learn to look at the world from that perspective. That new view helps them become more sensitive to others . . . and true to their feelings.

Teachable Moment

George came crying to his mother one day because Debbie had told her friend that he had wet the bed until last year. After empathizing with George and talking him into going outside to play, Britt sought out Debbie. "I understand you told your friend about George's bed-wetting problem. How do you suppose that made him feel?"

"I don't know," Debbie answered. "I guess it made him feel bad."

"I'm sure it did. By telling that private information, you broke the trust that your brother had in you to keep that problem in the family. George is your brother, and he deserves your loyalty. Because you did something that hurt him, you'll have to make it up to him by doing his chores for him today."

Teach children to take care of their environment. "All roads lead to home" is an old adage with quite a bit of truth in it. When children invest themselves in their surroundings, they are demonstrating loyalty to their community. Show your children ways they can take care of their home, their school, and their community in general. Tell them how much longer things will last when they are properly cared for, and how defacing things not only costs money to repair but destroys them and, in so doing, their possibility of others' enjoying them, too.

Teachable Moment

When the children commented about graffiti and trash in the local park, the Porters decided that they could demonstrate community loyalty by making cleaning up the park their family project. On Saturday, they all took trash bags to the park and proceeded to clean up as much of the park as they could. After a long, tiring day, they sat on a park bench with several bags of their hard work stacked up beside them and enjoyed looking at their clean park.

"We owed this clean park to everyone," Brill remarked. "Now I hope everyone will help keep it clean so we can keep enjoying it."

This demonstration of community loyalty was something the Porters were certain their children would remember; it was not only hard work but work that brought the family closer together and closer to their community as well.

Help children establish strong family connections. Family loyalty results when children feel connected to their own unique family. To help your children feel this bond, teach them about their family roots — how they are connected to their extended family. Family quarrels and feuds create a loyalty dilemma for children who are being asked to choose sides. Avoid this pitfall of family life by allowing them to be privy to knowing your family's "who's who" without any editorializing from you about past relationships your family has had with its members.

WARNING: AVOID ASKING CHILDREN TO CHOOSE SIDES.

Frequently, children of divorced families are asked with whom they would like to live. Such a question forces them to choose one parent over the other or one family over the other. Rather than force a choice, an outside authority should make the decision based on the best interests of the children.

Teachable Moment

One day at dinner, George asked, "Who is Chuck?"

"Oh, you must mean your cousin," Britt answered.

"Yeah, that guy who's graduating from high school," George said eagerly.

"Well, he's my brother Jim's son," Britt offered. "My brother is your uncle, and his children are cousins of yours."

"Then can we go to the graduation? I want to meet him. I didn't know I had a cousin named Chuck."

"No, we can't go. They live clear across the country, but we'll send a gift," Britt answered.

"But is he still our cousin since Uncle Jim got divorced?" George asked.

"Yes, because Jim is still my brother, so he is still your uncle and any of his children are your cousins."

"Boy, is this confusing!" George said as he changed the subject.

Britt and Dave agreed that they needed to talk more about their family with their children in order to help their children understand their family connections. Even they sometimes got people mixed up!

Get a pet. Having a pet that your children must feed and take care of is an amazing ticket to a show of loyalty. Not only can caring for pets show how to be loyal, but some pets are excellent models of loyalty as they stand by their owners through thick and thin.

"I never really knew what being loyal was until I had a dog. Now that I have a dog, I have a true responsibility and I show her that true sense of loyalty by giving her the care she needs." —KATIE

Teachable Moment

When Debbie finally got the puppy that she had been hoping to hold and love for years, there were just two conditions: She would be in charge of the "day" care and her stepdad would help with her housebreaking chores at night. It was amazing to see the genuine love and loyalty that developed almost immediately between the puppy and her human mom — the most wonderful lesson in loyalty this family could ever have devised.

"Charity is the bone shared with the dog when you are just as hungry as the dog." —JACK LONDON

COURTESY

"Life is not so short but that there is always time enough for courtesy." — RALPH WALDO EMERSON

cour·te·sy *n.* **1.** excellence of manners or social conduct; polite behavior **2.** a courteous, respectful, or considerate act or expression **3.** indulgence, consent, or acquiescence **4.** favor, help, or generosity

○ "Oh! I'm sorry. That was thoughtless of me."

○ "Excuse me. I didn't mean to crowd into line in front of you."

○ "Thank you so much for your help."

○ "I got a card and check from Grandma. I'm going to send a thank-you note right now."

THESE "SACRAMENTS OF CONSIDERATION" called courtesy are *absolutely* important to the smooth functioning of our society. Those who are considerate enough to think of the needs of others and to be courteous increase the pleasantness of everyday life and reduce its conflicts, thus reducing the pollution of violence around them.

This "law of reciprocity" implies that people get back what they give. That would mean, then, that courtesy begets courtesy. If this is true, then why isn't there less rudeness and more common courtesy when people interact with each other? We are indeed suffering from a courtesy famine; please feed the hungry and discover how good it feels!

WHAT DO WE MEAN BY COURTEOUS?

- ° Courteous people are aware of the feelings of others.
- ° Manners are used by courteous people to smooth social interaction.
- ° Being polite even in the face of rudeness: That is the sign of courtesy.
- ° Considerate, generous people enjoy being civil to one another.

MEET THE TILSON FAMILY

Largo and Matt Tilson became aware of the need to teach courtesy to their nine-year-old son, Rick, and seven-year-old son, Rob, when they heard Rick being rude to someone on the telephone. When confronted with the problem, Rick simply said, "It was just some guy trying to sell something." The Tilsons knew from this brief example that their task was going to be a formidable one, for they had heard other comments like it from Rick and were aware of the rampant rudeness they all witnessed daily on TV. They had even heard their sons and their friends being absolutely barbarian in their conversations, and then heard those same comments spewing forth like so much venom from a video they had innocently rented for the family. Courtesy seemed to be a distant and unattainable goal, but they were determined to try to reach it for the sake of their family's harmony and that of the world outside their home.

Teaching Tools

Mediate TV. Children today learn much of their social behavior from what they watch on TV. Even if your child doesn't see the behavior being modeled, his friends may imitate it so that all of their friends — your children included — can mimic it. This socialization by TV can have its good side, but often rudeness and sarcasm are being modeled rather than courtesy and manners. In order to neutralize the effects of the negative models your children are exposed to from TV, it is important to watch what your children watch and discuss with them the lessons they may be learning.

WARNING: DON'T OVERREACT TO A LACK OF COURTESY IN YOUR CHILDREN.

Without clear rules about manners, children might not understand the subtleties of courtesy. When they make mistakes and use poor manners, it's important to simply remind them about the rules and how to carry them out. Becoming angry and punishing children for their lack of manners only creates anger and resentment, and reduces the probability that children will want to follow the example of the punishing adult.

Teachable Moment

Largo walked into the family room while Rick and Rob were watching TV, and she overheard the boys laughing and repeating the phrase "It's the economy, stupid!" to each other.

"What are you guys watching?" she asked.

"It's the TV, stupid," Rick answered, and the boys erupted in a fit of laughter.

"That really hurts me when you call me stupid," Largo retorted. "And I'm not going to allow you to talk to me or anyone else like that."

"Gee, Mom. I didn't mean anything by it," Rick apologized. "It was funny when they said it on TV."

"Just because it's on TV doesn't mean you can say it to anybody else. Calling people mean names is never funny to the person you're attacking, even though it may sound funny to those around him," Largo said.

"I'm sorry, Mom! We won't do it again. I didn't mean to hurt your feelings," Rick answered, guilt written all over his face.

Realizing the impact of his behavior taught Rick a lesson he can use all his life: What we say and do *does* have an impact on others' hearts and souls.

Model courtesy. Children learn best when they see the specific lessons modeled right before their very eyes. Why? Because seeing certain behavior forms a concrete image in children's minds, which makes it easier for them to act out what they have witnessed. You may see your children mimicking many inappropriate behaviors they have seen others do, ranging from name-calling to martial-arts games. That's not surprising, because research on violence supports the contention that children repeat what they see — for better or for worse.

This aspect of learning makes it essential that you demonstrate courteous behavior whenever you can so that your children will have a positive model to follow when they have to choose whether to be "rude" or "nice" to others. Make it your responsibility to be the courtesy role model you know your children need in order to ensure their being exposed to the civil ways of socializing by those whom they respect the most.

WARNING: AVOID BEING DISCOURTEOUS.

Sometimes in exasperation, you may find yourself being discourteous to your children as well as to others. If your patience and self-discipline wear so thin that they are sometimes nonexistent, apologize to your children and talk to them about how the problem could have been solved in a more courteous way.

Teachable Moment

While at a shopping mall with the boys, Largo ran into a family acquaintance.

"Oh my!" the woman squealed with delight. "What handsome boys you have, dear."

"Why, thank you," Largo answered politely. "Say hello to Mrs. Smithers, boys!"

"Hello," they mumbled as they tried in vain to hide behind their mother.

Mrs. Smithers talked and talked and talked while Largo smiled and nodded and answered where appropriate. But after a while, she began to get restless.

"You must excuse us, Mrs. Smithers," Largo finally interjected. "We have got a ton of shopping to do before we have to meet Matt. He hates us being late!" And they hurried off as soon as they could.

"Mom, Mrs. Smithers talks a lot, doesn't she?" Rob observed.

"Yes, she does like to talk," Largo answered. "I was afraid we'd be late if she talked much longer."

"Why didn't we just walk off?" Rick asked.

"That wouldn't be very polite, would it?" Largo answered. "How would you feel if you were talking to me and I just walked off?"

"I guess I wouldn't like it," Rick answered.

"I think we need to treat people with courtesy no matter what," Largo continued. "That way *we* are more likely to be treated with courtesy."

Even though the encounter with Mrs. Smithers delayed them in their shopping, Largo was glad to have had the opportunity to show the boys that people can treat others with courtesy even if it is inconvenient. "Good manners are never expensive," she remembered her mother saying to her when she was a little girl.

"One thing I always try to accomplish is being courteous to the people around me. It's always nice to have them make nice comments back about you, and then you have a good reputation, on top of it." — KATIE

Teach manners. Good manners are important social graces, often overlooked today, that establish a caring environment in which to work and play. In fact, manners are truly the basic tools that people use to avoid offending each other. By teaching your children good manners and reinforcing them, you can be sure that they have the tools to use to get along well with others, without using a lawyer to intervene because someone confused a lack of manners with illegal behavior!

WARNING: AVOID USING TANGIBLE REWARDS FOR COURTESY.

Using sticker charts seems like a good idea in order to reward children for appropriate behavior. But when tangible rewards are used consistently, children come to expect them for everything. Rather than using stickers or other material rewards, praise the appropriate behavior by describing what you see happening. "You used your telephone manners very nicely" and "Thank you for chewing your food with your mouth closed" are examples of descriptive praise that keeps the "good manners" goal in front of your children without building their expectation that they should get a reward every time they do something you like.

Teachable Moment

From the time when their children were younger, the Tilsons had tried to instill good manners in them by using good manners themselves. They laid out the manners mandates and tried to reinforce them whenever they saw good manners. Dinner table rules were the ones most frequently exercised and reinforced. Typical dinner conversation was punctuated by such statements as, "You are keeping your hand and your napkin in your lap so nicely," "Thank you for remembering to chew with your mouth closed," "You asked for more salad so politely," and "You said please and thank you. That's great!"

Largo recognized the need for even further manners training when she overheard Rick answer the telephone. "He's not here now," Rick said, and hung up.

"Rick, who was the call for?" Largo asked.

"Dad. But I told the man he wasn't here."

"Yes, I heard that. It would have been more polite if you had said it differently, though," Largo explained.

"What else did I need to say?" Rick asked.

"Go get your brother, please. I think it's time to work on telephone manners," Largo said, and she went to the desk and got out some index cards. On a card, she wrote the following:

- Tilson residence, _____ speaking.
- Just a moment, please, I'll get her/him.
- I'm sorry. He/she's not available right now. May I take a message?

After she wrote the statements on a card, she gave it to the boys. "This will be by the telephone, and it tells you how we want you to answer. This is how your dad and I answer, and we'd like you to do the same. Now let's practice."

The boys spent the next few minutes pretending to answer the phone and responding to her as if she were a caller. "Doesn't it feel good to know what to say when people call? If I think of new things to put on the card, we can practice some more," Largo concluded, knowing that teaching appropriate behavior was far more valuable than getting angry about inappropriate antics.

"The test of good manners is to be able to put up pleasantly with bad ones." — ANONYMOUS

1 1

PATIENCE

"You have to accept whatever comes, and the only important thing is that you meet it with courage and with the best you have to give."
— ELEANOR ROOSEVELT

pa·tient *adj.* **1.** bearing pains or trials calmly without complaint **2.** manifesting forbearance under provocation or strain **3.** not hasty or impetuous **4.** steadfast despite opposition, difficulty, or adversity **5.** able or willing to bear
pa·tience *n.* the capacity, habit, or fact of being patient

- "That's okay, Mom. I can do without those really expensive shoes."

- "I'm hungry, but I can wait for dinner, Mommy."

- "Some kids called me names at school today, but I can handle it."

- "I failed the math test today. Guess I need to study harder."

PATIENCE CAN BE DIFFICULT for children to develop and use. If they have learned few coping skills to put into play when faced with adversity, they will become frustrated quickly. When children are told they can't have something or that they have to delay getting what they think they need, many "go off," throwing tantrums and demanding that the world revolve around their plan of action — *now!* To help children develop patience and learn to tolerate frustration and adversity, it is important for them not to get their way all the time, and to experience low-risk struggles which force them to learn how to handle confusion and disappointment, two unfortunate facts of life that call for patience.

WHAT DO WE MEAN BY PATIENCE?

- Learning to delay wants is part of developing patience.
- Planning for future goals demonstrates that a child can tolerate frustration and adversity.
- Children who have learned to be patient know how to take the steps needed to reach goals.
- Understanding that they can't always have what they want and that they aren't necessarily entitled to everything is essential in developing the virtue called patience.

"Don't run your pants off, it'll be your turn soon."
— BRAD

MEET THE CARLOS FAMILY

Joe and Marie Carlos were faced with the need to teach their children, three-year-old Carlita and ten-year-old Joe, Jr., to tolerate frustration when Junior had a tantrum because he couldn't have super-expensive athletic shoes. After the screaming and crying had subsided, Joe and Marie tried to reason with Junior, but to no avail. He claimed to hate his parents because they wouldn't let him have what he said he so desperately needed (but really just wanted). Joe and Marie realized that Joe, Jr., had never learned the lessons of patience, and through this simple exercise of meeting needs, not wants, he was beginning to increase his ability to endure future frustrations of life.

TEACHING TOOLS

Teach goal-setting. Children who can set goals and understand the steps needed to reach the goals are more likely to be patient while they wait to get what they want. When children ask to have or do certain things, instead of your automatically telling them yes or now, ask them how they think they might go about getting what they want. If they have no clue as to a means to their coveted end, help them outline the steps.

Teachable Moment

When Junior had a tantrum about the shoes that he wanted but couldn't have, Joe and Marie waited for the screaming and crying to subside, and then they started to help him set a goal.

"If we can't buy the expensive shoes for you, how could you get the money for them yourself?" Joe asked.

"You should buy them for me!" Junior demanded.

"We can't afford to do that, but we do have enough money to buy shoes that cost about half of that amount. So you only have to come up with half the money to get the other ones. Now, how can you do that?"

"You could just give it to me," Junior answered defiantly.

"I'm sorry I'm not making myself clear. Here are the choices you have: We will buy a pair of shoes that cost less than those you want, or you can earn the money we don't have, pay for the difference, and get the shoes you want. I think you should take a while to decide what you want to do," Joe said.

After a few days of thinking about the problem and discussing it with the help of his parents, Junior decided that he could earn money by doing odd jobs for neighbors, mowing lawns, raking leaves, running errands, and other things. When he had earned the money, he decided he didn't want the shoes after all! They weren't worth all the hard-earned sweat he had put into working for the money.

Make children work for what they want. Children who work for privileges develop a greater appreciation for what they have and what they are allowed to do. Following Grandma's Rule — when you have done what you have to do, then you get to do what you want to do — children learn to delay gratification and know that what they want comes only with effort and patience.

WARNING: DON'T GIVE CHILDREN AN ALLOWANCE.

Children who are given an allowance learn to get something for nothing. Even if an attempt to tie allowance to chores or duties is made, children rarely make the connection that the money they're given is for what they have done. Rather than receiving an allowance, they should be expected to take care of their rooms and make their beds, for example, simply because they are a part of the family. Children should also be expected to help with such family chores as setting the table, feeding pets, and helping with dinner. Rather than giving an allowance, choose large jobs that must be done weekly and pay children for the proper completion of those jobs. Sweeping, dusting, cleaning bathrooms, and other major cleaning duties that are generally done on a weekly basis can be a good source of income for all children.

Teachable Moment

Joe and Marie developed a plan for their children to try to teach them that they had to work before they played. To remind themselves and the children of the new rule, they made a sign for the refrigerator door that said, "When you have . . . , then you may . . ."

When Carlita came into the kitchen to ask for a snack, Marie said, "I'd love to get you a snack. When you have picked up the toys you were playing with and put them where they belong, then you may have a snack."

Carlita fussed and whined, but Marie stuck to the new rule, and the toys were put away. Both Marie and Joe were pleased that they had found a way not only to get their children to do things they needed to do but also to help them develop the patience to delay doing what they wanted until their work was done.

Teach children how to wait. Children who learn to wait for what they want have a chance to develop patience and tolerance for frustration. To teach children to wait, you must give them practice in waiting as well as directions on what they can do while waiting.

WARNING: AVOID GIVING IN TO WHINING.

When children are frustrated, they often resort to whining, and parents are likely to give in just to stop the obnoxious noise. Rather than giving in to the inappropriate behavior, give children empathy for their suffering, but stand fast to your rule (about which they are probably whining) so that they don't learn that whining will get them what they want.

Teachable Moment

When Marie was on the telephone, Carlita decided that she needed help with what she was doing, and she demanded that her mother get off the phone to help her. "I'm sorry," her mother said, "I'm on the phone right now and can't help you."

Unfortunately, Carlita began to scream and cry in order to get her mother to attend to her needs. Marie quickly ended her conversation and took Carlita to time-out.

When time-out was over, she said, "I'm sorry I can't do what you want the minute you want it. When I'm busy on the phone, I just can't stop and take care of you, unless it is an emergency. So here's what we'll do. I'm going to put these markers and this paper in the drawer by the phone. If you need something and I'm on the phone, I'll open this drawer and get the markers and paper out, and you can sit here by me and draw until I'm off the phone. That way you'll have something fun to do while you wait."

By solving the problem with a positive alternative to nagging her while she is on the phone, Marie knew she was teaching a double lesson: Whining doesn't pay and creative solutions can often help everyone's needs be met.

"When I was seven, my parents bestowed upon me a bedtime that I felt was nothing short of criminal. I was frustrated, but I remembered what my parents told me: Control your temper instead of throwing a fit. I politely asked them if they could allow me another hour of daily activity and they said yes!" —CLARE

Allow low-risk failure. If children are protected from any risk of failure, they won't gain experience in learning how to handle the consequences of their decisions. You can help your child with failure tolerance by giving him the opportunity to fail! Allowing low-risk failures, such as failing to get to watch TV because their toys didn't get picked up on time, gives children experience in how to cope with disappointment and how to patiently handle not getting to do what they want when they want to.

WARNING: DON'T RESCUE CHILDREN FROM FAILURE.

In order for children to learn how to be patient and cope with frustration and adversity, they must experience failure. That is not to say that they must fail a grade in school or permanently scar themselves, but they should be exposed to life's little failures. For example, if your child forgets to take his homework to school, he must suffer the consequences at school without being rescued by your bringing the homework to school for him. During this failure experience, be caring and empathic so that your child has support, but don't take the consequences away. Without dealing with consequences and the minor suffering that accompanies it, children will have difficulty in learning to cope with frustration and adversity, an experience that teaches them patience and living with their decisions.

Teachable Moment

Marie and Joe were tired of fighting with their children about their getting ready for bed, so they decided to start a bedtime routine. They used a timer to play "Beat the Clock," and they required Carlita and Junior to meet certain goals in order to stay up and play until bedtime.

The first night, neither of the children beat the clock getting their pajamas on an hour before their normal bedtime, so they were put to bed early. The next night, they raced so fast to beat the clock that they almost crashed together, but they made it and were able to stay up for the hour before their normal bedtime. Failure not only motivated them to hurry getting themselves ready but also gave them a lesson in how to tolerate and accept themselves — imperfections and all.

Teach empathy. One way for children to learn to cope with frustration and adversity and develop patience is to teach them how to have empathy for others. In order for your children to learn empathy, they must first learn to put themselves in others' shoes and to learn to think about what those others are going through that could be affecting their behavior, language, or mood, for example. This ability to understand the needs of other people can help divert attention from your child's own frustrations, as well as help him understand why a person does or says something that may be frustrating those around him.

Teachable Moment

Junior came home from school and announced that there was a new boy in his class. "The teacher said that he was from special education, and I know he's excused from reading group because he can't read. She said he was part of something called inclusion, I think. Mom, what's special education and inclusion?"

"That's where children who have trouble learning go to the same school you do, but they get the special help they need," Marie answered. "We got something from school that said they were going to start including children from special education classes in regular classes with other children. I guess that's what inclusion means."

"Why do they have trouble learning? Doesn't everybody learn stuff like me and Carlita?" asked Junior.

"No, sweetheart, everybody doesn't learn the same. Some kids have problems hearing and listening, some have problems seeing, and some just have problems learning to read or learning math."

Junior was troubled by his mother's revelation. "You mean some kids are just dumb, don't you?"

Marie could see that she needed to be more specific and to the point. "No, Junior, some children have learning disabilities, but they aren't dumb. And some are blind or deaf or any number of things, so that they need more help than other kids. That's why they're in special education."

Marie could almost see the wheels turning in his head as Junior thought about what she had said. "You know, Mom, I was really mad because I had to do my homework and you made me read a half hour every day. But Tommy can't even read. I really feel bad that I made such a fuss over something that's not very important."

The next day when he came home from school, Junior announced that he had a new friend. "Tommy and I are friends. I thought about him not being able to read, and I decided that he needed someone who could help him."

Marie was so proud that she cried.

"Why are you crying, Mom?" Junior asked, troubled.

"I feel so sorry for Tommy that he has problems learning to read; and I'm so proud of you, Junior, for wanting to be his friend. That is so thoughtful of you."

And she was proud. Her son had shown that he could feel compassion for someone who was different. His level of caring and empathy for the needs of others was something to celebrate.

Help children cope with disappointment. Like all of us, children are faced with disappointment every day, and many simply don't know how to handle the emotional letdown. As a result, these children have tantrums, verbally attack their parents, and may become depressed. At the core of this inability to cope with disappointment is the children's thinking. Those who think that not getting what they want will be a disaster of insurmountable proportions will not be able to cope with disappointment. In order to help your children learn to cope with disappointment, teach them how to "reformat" situations so that these situations aren't disasters but rather only disappointing events. By telling children that they can handle any problem that comes their way and helping them project beyond their immediate disappointment, you will be able to guide them into learning to cope with one of life's most difficult challenges — the inevitable times when things don't go their way.

Teachable Moment

"I want to stay and play longer!" Carlita whined when Marie told her that they had to leave a friend's house. "I never get to do what I want to do."

"We've been here long enough, and we need to go now," Marie insisted, but Carlita increased the noise level. Marie was about to begin yelling herself, but she got herself under control.

"I understand how you feel. You want to stay and play, but we simply can't. Now, let me tell you what your choices are: You can go now and then come back and play some other time, or you can tell yourself that this is an awful and terrible thing to have happen and be so upset that you can't stand it. When you make yourself so mad, then you do things that get you into trouble. Now, what do you want to do? Do you want to get mad and not be able to come back, or tell yourself that you had a good time and leave now so you can come back later?"

Carlita decided that it would be better to leave now and come back to play on another day. Marie was pleased with her daughter's decision-making and with her increasing ability to have patience for things that she thought were frustrating . . . a lesson even Marie sometimes had to learn anew, too.

When you say no, stick to it. When parents refuse children's requests, they must be willing to stick to their guns regardless of the potential onslaught of begging, wheedling, whining, and cajoling that might follow their saying no. Being able to continue to refuse to give your child permission to do something or go somewhere in the face of such persistence takes great strength and resolve. To help your child tolerate "no," you should not only be willing to stick to your decision but also make continuing to badger you about it "expensive" by charging one job for each minute it continues.

Teachable Moment

Junior wanted to go to a friend's house, but he had family chores that hadn't been done, and Marie was determined to make sure that his work was finished before he left the house.

"But I promise," Junior begged. "I'll do them when I get back. Please, won't you let me go? Please! Please! Please!"

"I'm sorry, Junior," Marie countered calmly. "The rule

is that you have to do all your chores before you can go anyplace."

"But it's only for a little while," Junior began again, but Marie cut him off.

"The answer is still no. And I'll tell you what. Arguing and begging me isn't going to help. But if you want to continue, I'll sell you the right to do so for a job a minute."

"What do you mean, a job a minute?" Junior asked, suddenly curious.

"I mean that for every minute you keep begging, I'll give you another job to do for me. You can beg as long as you choose."

Junior stared at his mother for a few moments, then turned and left the room. Thirty minutes later, he announced that his chores were done. After Marie inspected them to make sure they were done well, she let him go to his friend's. She was proud of herself for being able to stick to her principles and invoke the rule about doing chores before any fun activities could be done, and Junior felt good, too, about doing what he knew was right. He hated admitting that getting his work done before he played seemed so reasonable to him!

Help children learn to tolerate siblings. Children often express an intolerance for their siblings by fighting with them, putting them down, or even ignoring their presence. For the sake of good mental health and harmony for the family, children can learn to have patience for their siblings' behavior. To teach your children sibling tolerance, make it a family rule that they get along with each other. Once the rule is set, praise your children for getting along, and give negative consequences when they choose not to do so.

WARNING: AVOID ALLOWING CHILDREN TO SAY THEY "CAN'T STAND" THINGS.

When people say that they can't stand something, they are discounting their own internal strength and ability to withstand adversity. Children who practice saying, "I can't stand it!" not only close the door to being able to put up with things they don't like, but they also put themselves down, which decreases their ability to approach challenges positively.

Teachable Moment

"You little creep!" Junior shouted. "You're standing in front of the TV just to bug me. Now *move*! Mom, would you come get your daughter!"

"I'm sorry you've chosen to not get along," Marie said as she entered the room. She knew that she shouldn't solve this problem for Junior and that both children were responsible for getting along with each other. "Because you have chosen not to get along, Carlita, you have to go to time-out. (For the definition of time-out, please turn to page 50.) Junior, I want you to vacuum the family room. When you are through, you both need to decide whether you want to get along or take more time-out and do more jobs."

"But she was deliberately trying to bother me!" Junior tried to explain.

But Marie reminded him of the rule about getting along. Later she tried to help Junior with problem-solving his little sister's irritating behavior.

"I can't stand it when she does that!" he told his mother. "She just drives me crazy!"

Not much of a "drive," Marie was tempted to say, but

instead she said, "I think you can stand more than you believe you can. You're giving that little girl a lot of power over you. Instead of just believing that you can't stand her behavior, think of ways you might handle her when she's being a pest."

"I'll waste her," Junior answered sullenly.

"And what do you think might happen if you do?" Marie asked calmly.

"You'd waste me!" Junior answered emphatically. "I guess I could offer to play with her."

"Now, that's being creative." Marie was enthusiastic. "You have a lot of power over Carlita. She thinks you're the greatest. All you need to do is be nice to her, and she'll be nice back. I think you can stand that."

"Yeah, Mom," Junior said. "I guess I can stand a lot more than I think I can. All I need to do is change my head a little bit."

Marie was proud of Junior's insight. Some days she was really disgusted with his behavior, but she knew that she could stand it!

"The greatest source of happiness is forgetting yourself and trying seriously and honestly to be useful to others." — MILLICENT FENWICK

1 2

RESOURCEFULNESS

"The question is not whether we will die, but how we will live." — JOAN BORYSENKO

re·source·ful *adj.* able to deal skillfully and promptly with new situations, difficulties, etc.

○ "I didn't know how to get the lid off this jar, but I decided I was turning it the wrong way and then, like magic, it opened!"

○ "We got mad at each other, but we worked it out."

○ "I didn't know how to work this math problem, so I looked at one like it and figured it out."

○ "I was hungry and you were on the phone, so I got myself a snack."

PROBLEMS ARE ALL RELATIVE — particularly when they are faced by families. From day to day, a child's definition of a problem may change like the wind. So when parents see that their child is struggling with a problem, however inconsequential it may seem to them, they need to take it seriously and help him try to work it out.

These lessons in problem-solving and resourcefulness can begin as early as preschool age because it is then that a child's desires and dreams may first butt heads with the enemy — reality. Although most parents would love to shield their offspring from life's disappointments and solve all of their problems for them, their children's path to independence is paved with problem-solving skills. The earlier children get practice in using these skills, the easier it will be for them to move forward positively on the resourceful road to self-sufficiency and self-reliance in adulthood.

"If I have a problem that I don't understand, I go back, read it all over again, take a deep breath, and try again." — NIKKI

WHAT DO WE MEAN BY PROBLEM-SOLVING?

- Problems are barriers that prevent people from reaching their goals.
- To solve problems, the limitations of individual power must be recognized.
- To become independent and self-sufficient, problem-solving must be learned.
- Problem-solving involves a set of skills that can be learned, practiced, and refined.

MEET THE MEDVED FAMILY

Ralph and Natilie Medved found themselves telling their three boys, four-year-old Zach, six-year-old Evan, and ten-year-old Barry, how to solve every problem that came along. They soon realized that the boys were becoming increasingly dependent on them to remove all the barriers that ever stood in their way so that life would be as smooth as glass. Realizing that this parenting habit would be hard to break, the parents tried to change their behavior by teaching their children how they could think through the problems that were a daily part of their lives instead of being rescued from any familiarity with failure. By teaching their children how to come up with solutions that drew them closer to meeting their goals, the whole family was rewarded with more independence and feelings of self-confidence.

TEACHING TOOLS

Model problem-solving. Imagine that your children are young sponges who are soaking up your behavior (bad and good!). Then look at the ways that you solve problems and make reasonable decisions based on your conclusions. Talk through these problem-solving steps whenever you have a problem so that your offspring can see how much cooler and calmer these steps can help a person feel when he is in the midst of a social heatstroke:

1. List all possible solutions.
2. Decide the consequences of each.
3. Choose the solution with the positive consequences that leads you closest to your goal.

WARNING: AVOID LOSING YOUR COOL IN THE FACE OF A CRISIS.

Children learn by example, so keeping your cool when everyone around you is losing his is an important way to help children learn to problem-solve. If you feel panic setting in, take a moment to regain a sense of calm by telling yourself that you can handle whatever comes your way. Setting a good model for your children will pay big dividends later.

Teachable Moment

Pacing back and forth in her dining room, Natilie found herself wondering out loud how she was going to get Evan to school and still be on time for the dentist appointment she had made for Zach, since the two events occurred at the same time. When she looked up, she saw both boys looking expectantly at her. Now was the time to show them how to go about solving problems, she decided.

"Well, let's see now," she began, "we could keep Evan home from school. What about that, Evan? Would that be a good way to solve the problem?"

"No! I'll miss a whole bunch of stuff," Evan answered immediately.

"Well, then, what about calling the dentist and canceling Zach's appointment?"

This time it was Zach who answered. "No! I'll get cavities!"

Natilie smiled. It was nice to see that the talk about brushing teeth and visiting the dentist regularly had been heard. "Well, maybe we could call Jake's mother, Marge, to see if she would take Evan to school so we can go to the dentist," she said to Zach.

"Yeah, that's a good idea," Evan crowed. "Then I can ride to school with Jake. He's cool. He lets me play with the rest of the third graders sometimes at recess."

Natilie called Marge, and she agreed to pick Evan up on her way to take Jake to school. What a relief! Natilie thought. If I keep my cool, I can think of solutions better than if I get upset; and by doing so, I can teach my children to avoid going crazy when they need to make decisions. Not only had this solved the problem of her needing to be in two places at once, but it also gave her an opportunity to model problem-solving for her sons.

Talk children through their own problem-solving. When your children come to you with problems, rather than giving them solutions, talk them through the process by asking questions. In this way they learn to brainstorm possible solutions and are more likely to follow through with the one they choose, since *they* were the architects.

WARNING: AVOID RESCUING CHILDREN.

When children are faced with problems, parents are often tempted to take over and solve the problems for them. This form of rescue develops children's dependence on their parents by putting them in the role of a "safety net," instead of a "guide" to helping children find solutions to problems.

Teachable Moment

One day when he came home from work, Ralph heard a commotion in Evan's room. When he went in, Evan was threatening to hit Zach. "What's the problem?" the boys' concerned father asked.

Evan whined that Zach had been in his room playing in his stuff while he was at school. "I don't want him in here messing up my things. Make him stay out, Dad!" Evan pleaded.

"Let's see if we can figure out a way to solve this problem," Ralph began. "Now, what could you do to keep him from playing with your things?"

"I'll beat him up every time he comes in here and gets in my stuff," Evan answered with obvious pleasure.

"Well, if you do that, what do you think would happen?" Ralph asked.

"He'll stay out of my stuff!" Evan squealed with relish.

"What bad thing might happen if you beat him up?" Ralph asked ominously.

"Oh," Evan answered. "I get it. I'd get in real trouble, wouldn't I?"

"Yes, I think you would," Ralph continued seriously. "What else could you do?"

"I need a lock on my door," Evan answered.

"Where would you keep the key?" Ralph asked. "And what if you lost it?"

"I could keep it on a string around my neck. Bobby has the key to his house on a string around his neck. And you could keep one of the keys hidden in the kitchen so if I lost it we could still unlock the door."

"That's good thinking, but it's very possible that your mother or I might need to go into your room while you're not here. I don't think we'd want to go get the key each time," Ralph answered. "What else can we do?"

"Maybe we could lock my closet. That way I could put my good stuff in there, and Zach couldn't get it," Evan continued.

"That sounds like a good idea to me. I have a door lock on my workbench. Let's put it on your closet right now," Ralph answered, pleased to have been able to talk Evan through the problem.

"You have to be smarter than the problem you are solving. Patience is one major characteristic that is needed. With that, the answer is left at your feet and all you have to do is to try to pick it up." —WADE

Encourage independence. When children act independently, they are demonstrating their ability to solve problems. Sometimes, however, parents discourage their budding independence because they think their children won't be able to be successful at accomplishing their goal. When your children attempt to do something themselves, encourage them when it is a safe risk to do so, even if they occasionally meet failure.

WARNING: AVOID TAKING OVER WHEN CHILDREN ENCOUNTER TROUBLE.

Messy though it may be at times, children need to learn independence through trial and error. When they prove that they can accept the responsibility of doing certain things, and have the skills to be able to solve many problems that they encounter along the way, that is the time to let go of a little more kite string, as you encourage their growth and self-reliance along their life flights.

Teachable Moment

Natilie was talking on the telephone when Zach came in wanting a glass of juice. She couldn't end the conversation yet, so she told him to wait. Not known for his patience, Zach disappeared into the kitchen. When Natilie finally hung up the phone and went into the kitchen, she found Zach with the floor mop busily trying to clean up the juice that he had spilled on the floor. Natilie's first impulse was to punish him for not waiting for her to help him, but she decided that she should help him with his quest for independence.

When Zach looked up, his face filled with panic, she said, "Would you like some help?"

"I'm sorry, Mommy. I didn't mean to spill, but it came out so fast and ran over the glass and on the floor."

"I know you didn't mean to spill. You could have waited for me to get off the phone, but you wanted to do it yourself. That way you could solve your own problem. And you're learning how to clean up if you make a mess."

By allowing him to help himself and to make mistakes in doing so, Natilie knew she was helping him learn to come up with solutions to meet his goals of independence and self-sufficiency — two goals Natilie wanted him to reach.

Ask questions. When parents act as the ultimate authority, children learn to depend on them to provide the answers to problems. Even if the solution your children may choose is not what you would like, allow them to discover their own errors by not rescuing them and solving the problem for them. If your children ask you questions about how to solve a problem, rather than giving quick and easy answers, ask questions that can lead them to discover the answers for themselves.

Teachable Moment

When Barry asked his dad why he had to go clean his room, Ralph was tempted to resort to the old authoritarian retort "Because I said so!" But he knew that Barry would only learn to take orders and not to think for himself if he used that line.

"Why do you think I asked you to clean your room?" he asked his son instead.

"I don't know," Barry whined. "To be mean, I guess."

"What do you suppose would happen if you never cleaned up in there?"

"I don't know," Barry answered again.

"Since you don't know yet, let's sit here while you think of some reasons," his father calmly suggested.

Barry soon realized that he wasn't going to get to go play until he had solved this problem and cleaned his room, so he began to think about why rooms need to be cleaned. "I guess if I didn't clean it up, after a while there would be so much junk in there I couldn't go in," Barry offered.

"Sounds like a good reason to me," Ralph responded with a smile. "Now, how about getting it done so you can go play," he added, confident that his keeping his cool had helped his son use a cool head, too, to solve *his* problem.

"If the only tool you have is a hammer, you tend to see every problem as a nail." —ABRAHAM MASLOW

13

PEACEMAKING

*"I keep my ideals, because in spite of everything I
still believe that people are really good at heart."*
—ANNE FRANK

peace *n.* **1.** the normal, nonwarring condition of a nation, a
group of nations, or the world **2.** a historical period during
which such a condition exists **3.** a state of harmony among
people or groups **4.** the freedom from disorder normal in a
community **5.** cessation of or freedom from any strife or
dissension

peace·mak·er *n.* one who makes peace as by reconciling
parties at variance

- "I'm sorry I got on your nerves. I'll try to be more thoughtful."

- "You hurt my feelings, but I'm sure you didn't mean to."

- "Mom, we were about to fight over who was going to go
  first, but we flipped a coin."

- "I guess I'll have to apologize. It was my fault."

"CONFLICT" IS SUCH AN innocent-sounding word for such
a menacing fact of human life. Because of different opinions, personal agendas, and individual needs and wants,

conflicts rear their ugly heads and almost inevitably result when more than one person is involved in making a decision. "Listen to others and they will listen to you" is one simple way of stating the process of resolving conflict peacefully through understanding everyone's position in a conflict and trying to negotiate a compromise, while being empathic to everyone's individual agenda. When a child learns how to get along with others — in times of agreement and disagreement — he learns much more than how to resolve differences peacefully. He also develops an ability to put himself in another person's place, the essential foundation for learning the behaviors of virtue.

"It takes a bigger man to admit his guilt." — ALEXANDRA

What Do We Mean by Peacemaking?

- Peacemaking involves carefully trying to understand the needs and wants of another person.
- Working toward a solution in which everyone is satisfied is satisfactory peacemaking.
- Using empathy when listening to others can avoid conflict.
- Being assertive about one's rights and position on a subject can help a person avoid getting angry and, therefore, avoid beginning a conflict.
- Realizing that a win-win result is preferable to a win-at-all-costs conclusion in group situations is a true sign of the peacemaker.

Meet the Perez Family

Hector and Rose Perez were painfully aware of the need for peacemaking when they were around their three children, twelve-year-old Manuel, nine-year-old Martin, and five-year-old Lucinda. The verbal warfare among the children seemed continuous and often fierce. The children seemed to generate conflict by the simple act of sharing space! Instead of getting angry themselves, the Perezes decided to begin a conflict management training program, which was patterned after a similar program Hector's office implemented.

TEACHING TOOLS

Model appropriate ways to resolve conflicts without violence. How do you resolve differences between you and your spouse or friends? Do you hold grudges, yell and scream and bang down the phone when you become angry at someone? Children learn best when they see their parents behave as they (the children) have been told to behave. When you find yourself in the inevitable position of being at odds with another person, use good conflict resolution strategies so your children can see how to approach conflict positively.

WARNING: DON'T USE AGGRESSION TO CONTROL CHILDREN.

Children who watch adults resolve conflicts with aggression and violence are more likely to use the same aggression in resolving their own conflicts. When you use corporal punishment, like hitting or spanking, you are teaching your children to use violence as a problem-solving tool.

Teachable Moment

Hector and Rose were arguing about whether to replace the sofa in the living room. Rose was tired of the shabby look of the old sofa, but Hector thought it was perfectly adequate as long as the children were as young as they were, because they were still learning how to respect others' property. To their surprise, they noticed that their children had become intrigued with the discussion and were hanging on their every word. Trying to become good role models, Hector and Rose began to listen more carefully to each other's arguments and to rephrase what they thought they heard the other say.

"Let me see if I understand what you said," Hector said. "You think we should get a better quality sofa now because our children are old enough to take better care of it."

"Yes, I think so," Rose answered.

"Maybe while we shop around to see what's available and what the prices are, we can count the number of times something gets spilled on this sofa or how often the children seem to be abusing it," Hector suggested.

"You mean you'll go along with the idea of buying a new one if we can prove the children can take care of it?" Rose asked.

"I think we can afford it if it isn't too expensive. As I said: If we're going to buy new furniture, I don't want them to destroy it."

"We can negotiate price later when we find out what the range is," Rose answered, pleased that they were able to resolve the conflict by postponing a final decision and by doing some research to see if a new sofa would survive the wear and tear of their family's normal use.

Teach children to manage their anger. Anger is the primary reason conflict fails to be resolved. When a person is angry, he is not open to reasoning or listening to another person's ideas. In fact, when anger builds, it's as if a person's brain shrinks! When a person is feeling most out of control, that's when his anger skyrockets. Instead of giving up and losing control, though, try to understand why you're angry at certain times and teach your children to also be introspective enough to do so. Then once you've figured out what the problem is, practice effective problem-solving. Begin this process by teaching children to isolate themselves when they get angry. Once isolated, they can calm themselves by saying these words: *smooth, calm, quiet,* and *soft.* When they say the words, encourage them to visualize something smooth, think about quiet, try to feel calmness, and think of something soft. When they feel calm, encourage them to think about their own "angry adventure" and to tell you their story. Problem-solving can then begin.

"Clean up the mess. Frustration and fury cannot resolve the conflict." — WADE.

Teachable Moment

When Rose heard a loud crash, she quickly went into the family room where nine-year-old Martin and his twelve-year-old brother, Manuel, were fighting about who was going to get to play the video game.

"I was here first!" Martin was yelling.

"Whoa!" Rose shouted above the din. "What's the problem here?"

"I wanted to play the video game, and Manny just took the controller away and started playing," Martin explained.

"But, Mom," Manuel began, "I'm going to basketball practice in a half hour, and Marty wouldn't let me play. He can play all the time I'm gone!"

"I was here first!" Martin rejoined. "He can't take the controller away, because I was here first."

"What do you guys think you can do about this problem?" Rose asked.

"He can let me play," Manuel began.

"I was here first," Martin continued.

"I'll tell you what," Rose said. "You can work this out or the video game is put away for the day and won't be available to anybody until tomorrow. What do you think you can do to solve this conflict?"

"How about letting me play until basketball practice, and you can go first for the rest of the week?" Manuel suggested.

"Yeah, but you have basketball practice every day at the same time. You'll want to go first every day anyway," Martin retorted.

"Okay, how about letting me play until practice every day, and you can play all day Saturday if you want?" Manuel countered.

"How about you get to play Saturday, and I get to go with you when you and your friends go to the video store at the shopping center Friday night," Martin returned.

"I don't know . . ." Manuel began. "I don't think my friends would like you hanging out with us. Maybe I can convince them that you won't bother us. Just don't come around if we're talking to some girls."

"Don't worry," Martin said. "I wouldn't want to be near them anyway!"

"Thanks, guys. I'm glad you worked this out. Remember, if the game causes a problem, then it goes into time-out," Rose said, glad that she had not rescued the children by solving the problem for them. She never would have come up with *their* solution!

Hold regular family meetings. When families have regular meetings to work out problems, children learn how to resolve conflicts within a meeting context. To develop a family meeting format for your family, set a time each week when all the family members are usually at home, such as Sunday afternoon at four. The chair of the meeting should rotate so that each family member has a chance at being the head of the meeting. Family members should be encouraged to bring problems to the weekly meeting. One rule that supports everyone: Whoever brings a problem to the meeting must also bring a suggested solution.

WARNING: DON'T INTERVENE AND RESOLVE CONFLICTS FOR CHILDREN.

When parents intervene and take over conflicts so that children are saved from having to resolve it themselves, the children won't learn the process of problem-solving. To avoid such intervention, use a questioning technique so that your children are forced to think through the issues and come up with their own solutions.

"Be the peacemaker in a difficult situation. When J get in a fight, J just walk away. Jt's not worth it."
— DAVID

Teachable Moment

"Family meeting time!" Rose said to the background music of the moans of her children. "Who's the chair this week?"

"Dad is," Lucinda said brightly.

"Who wants to bring a problem before this tribunal?" Hector asked solemnly.

"I do," Lucinda answered. "I have a problem that's driving me crazy!"

"What's the problem, sweetheart?" Hector said gently.

"I don't like it that Manny and Marty always get to do things that I don't get to do. It's not fair!" she answered.

"What do you suggest we do?" Hector asked, holding back his desire to gently explain the age difference and to try to convince her that she was too young to do the same things they did.

"I think you should change the rules so I could do everything they do," Lucinda answered with petulance.

"If we change the rules, how will that make a difference for you?" Hector asked.

"It'll be fair, then." Lucinda answered.

"What if it's never fair?" Hector queried.

"Then I'll be mad!"

"And if you're mad, then how will you be able to handle that?" Hector asked patiently.

"Maybe if I go to my room and listen to music, I'll forget about all this," Lucinda shot back.

"That's a good way to make your anger go away," Hector said. "I think that's a good thing to do when life isn't going your way."

Hector and Rose were pleased with their family meetings because of the learning that was taking place there. Their children were becoming much less demanding of each other and of them, because they now felt that they had the power to at least bring grievances before the entire group. They knew that before they left the meeting, the problem would be aired and solutions addressed.

Mediate television. The most constant source of inappropriate examples of conflict management come right into your home every day through your television set. In order to help children learn which conflict management strategies are appropriate and which are not, it is important to mediate what is being watched so that you can at least present an appropriate alternative.

Teachable Moment

Hector and the boys were watching a baseball game on television in which the pitcher almost hit the batter with a pitched ball, the batter charged the pitcher's mound, and a big fight erupted. Both of the boys seemed really excited about the fight and were disappointed when the umpires and managers broke it up.

"Why did the batter do that?" Hector asked in order to check out the level of understanding in his household.

"Because he was mad. The pitcher dusted him, and he wanted to show him he couldn't do that and get away with it," Manuel answered.

"Was that the right thing for him to do?" Hector asked.

"Sure!" Martin chimed in. "He can't get away with almost hitting the batter!"

"Could they have handled it in a different way?" Hector asked.

"I guess he could have ignored the pitch or told the umpire," Manuel answered.

"If he ignored or complained, then what might have happened?" their dad asked.

"Nothing, I guess," Manuel answered slowly. "But wouldn't the pitcher think he got away with something?"

"But what?" Hector asked. "And so what if he got away with something? It's just a game, and if he continues to dust off batters, he'll end up walking them and eventually lose the game."

"Yeah, I guess," Manuel answered. "It's not that big of a deal."

Hector was pleased that he was able to help his sons think through the TV version of resolving conflict. There were so many examples that they see every day of violent ways to end differences. He just hoped he would continue to help his sons turn to peaceful negotiation and reasoning instead of abusive means to conclude conflicts.

Teach the art of negotiation. One of the most frequently used tools of the peacemaker is that of negotiation. When two sides reach an impasse, the skillful negotiator is often able to move the parties toward a solution both can see as beneficial. Crucial to negotiation is to work toward a collaboration, a way both parties can work together to achieve a common goal, rather than toward a compromise in which both sides feel they have given up something. Working for the common good in peacemaking brings this virtue full circle as it helps others as well as oneself.

Teachable Moment

When their twelve-year-old, Manuel, wanted to take up the drums, Rose and Hector gave a choral response: "*No way!*"

"Why not?" Manuel shot back. "All the guys are getting instruments, and we want to start a band."

"You heard us," Hector responded. "We said no. Now, that's it."

Later in reflecting on Manuel's request, they saw this as a mixed blessing. They wanted their children to have an interest in music, but they had hoped for an instrument that wouldn't be quite as intrusive as drums. They didn't hear from Manuel for a while, but a few days later he approached them.

"Hey, can I talk to you guys a minute?" he asked. They were taken aback by his request. Generally, he just barged in and started talking. Asking their permission was something new. "About the drums, I've been thinking about why you probably don't want me to take drums. It's the noise, right?"

"Well, they would be kind of noisy," Hector replied.

"How about a guitar?" Rose proposed. "I'm sure you could be in a band or something if you played guitar."

"Everybody plays guitar," Manuel said with contempt. "If me and my friends start a band, we'll need a drummer. That's what I want to do — play the drums."

"I don't know," Hector mused. "Drum sets are pretty expensive, and we'd need some rules about practice — you know, where, when, and how much."

"Dad, I can earn the money," Manuel joined in eagerly. "I'm earning quite a bit mowing grass this summer, and I know this guy who wants to sell his set so he can get some better drums. He says they're good for a beginner."

"What about lessons?" Rose asked. "You'll need to learn how to play."

"Well, this guy with the drums said he'd show me the basic stuff to get me started, and he said that Mr. Lockhart at school, you know, the music teacher, he gives lessons. That's where this guy takes."

"Who is 'this guy'?" Hector asked, suddenly curious.

"Oh, he's a junior in high school who helps coach Eric's soccer team. He's real nice. He helped Eric work on his game so that he got good enough to be starting goalkeeper."

"What about practice?" Rose continued. "When would you practice?"

"I'll practice," Manuel responded. "Don't worry!"

"Yeah, we've heard that before," Hector answered. "We want more details. I'll tell you what: You work out a schedule for practice, clean out your room so you can get a set of drums in there, come up with a budget so we can see how much the drums are and how much money you'll need, and we'll see whether the plan will fly."

"Thanks, Mom and Dad!" Manuel said as he rushed off.

Rose and Hector felt good about their negotiation. Manuel was showing a lot of responsibility, and they believed he would be able to fulfill his part of the bargain. They could see how the discipline required of drum lessons and practice would be good for him, and they were getting that coveted interest in music they wanted.

"My parents have told me over and over that fighting is not worth it because someone always gets hurt. When resolving conflict with my brother and sister, we sit down and talk about how to resolve the conflict." — DUSTIN

Help children use empathy and caring in their efforts toward collaboration. To be able to resolve conflict peacefully, one must be able to see the position of the other side and to come to care about what happens to them as a result of the negotiation. When neither party in negotiation cares about what happens to the other, hostility is the most likely result. As caring increases, so do openness and cooperation, and the likelihood of both working together for the common good.

Teachable Moment

Martin and a friend were playing together with a construction set when they began to argue about what they were going to build. "You always want to build rockets and stuff," Martin was saying to his friend. "I want to build a castle or some kind of building."

"No, that's what we did last time," Lance, his friend, insisted. "You always want to build buildings, and that's boring."

"Well, it's *my* house, and if you're not going to play what I want, you can go home!" Martin answered angrily.

"Oh yeah. Make me!" Lance responded as he prepared to fight.

"Hi, guys! What's up?" Rose said from the doorway. She had been summoned by the raised voices and decided she'd better see what the problem was.

"He never wants to do what I want to," Martin said of his friend.

"When we're at my house, you always get to pick," came the angry reply. "My mother makes me do what my guests want to do."

"Maybe we can figure out a solution here," Rose began. "Let's calm down and think this through. Marty, you and Lance have been friends for a long time, haven't you?"

"Yeah, I guess," Martin said, looking at the floor.

"And you like playing with each other, right?" she continued.

"Yeah, most of the time," came the reply.

"Think about how Lance must feel right now. His best friend is really mad at him just because he wants to do one thing and the friend wants to do something else. How'd you feel if you were at his house and he wouldn't let you play what you want?"

"I'd probably get mad and come home," Martin mumbled.

"How do you suppose you might be able to work this out?" Rose asked.

"How about we build a space station and a rocket to go with it," Lance offered. "That way we'd both get to build what we want, and we'd get to play together some more, and neither one of us would be mad."

"Yeah, good idea!" Martin responded brightly. "I'll build the buildings while you work on the rocket and the launching pad."

After a long pause, Martin continued somewhat sheepishly, "I'm sorry I got mad at you, Lance. I guess it's fair to let you do what you want when you come here. You're the guest. I didn't think about how you'd feel if I got really selfish and only wanted to do my thing."

Rose was pleased that the boys were able to collaborate in their solution, since it turned out so well. She was sure that Martin would continue to consider the feelings of his friends when he played with them in the future.

"In this era of world wars, in this atomic age, values have changed. We have learned that we are the guests of existence, travelers between two stations. We must discover security within ourselves."
— BORIS PASTERNAK

14

SELF-RELIANCE

"No bird soars too high, if he soars with his own wings." — WILLIAM BLAKE

re·li·ance *n.* **1.** confident or trustful dependence **2.** something relied on

- "You seem to be having so much fun playing here by yourself."
- "I'm playing with my dolls. We're playing house."
- "I'd rather read my book than do anything in the whole world!"
- "I've been in my room drawing with my crayons."

WITH THE TOUCH OF a button, today's children can be effortlessly transported into a wide variety of fantasy worlds. The effort needed for them to think of ways to entertain themselves is so much more than many children want to expend that they lapse into more simple modes of dependency on others for their amusement and entertainment. In fact, even preschool-age organized sports teams have become such a prevalent pastime for children that it has all but erased the lazy nights of backyard croquet, badminton, and Wiffle ball.

"Just because you can, doesn't mean you should" is the

wise phrase to keep in mind when helping children realize that just because they *can* now watch television, listen to the radio, or play a video game twenty-four hours a day doesn't mean that that's the best use of their time. When children turn off easily accessible television "friends" and turn to real-life play that depends on their brainpower, not electricity, for its energy, their level of satisfaction and sense of accomplishment flourish.

What Do We Mean by Self-Reliance?

- ◦ To be self-reliant, it is necessary to have pleasant associations with activities that are self-generated.
- ◦ Children who are self-reliant are controlled by forces from within themselves rather than by those in the environment.
- ◦ To entertain himself, a child must use his own creativity and imagination.
- ◦ The need for immediate gratification must be put aside when a child chooses to rely on himself for what he needs.
- ◦ Activities that foster self-reliance should be readily available and should cost very little.

Meet the Mitchell Family

Linda, a single mom with an eight-year-old son, Ben, and a six-year-old daughter, Leslie, began to appreciate the need to teach her children self-reliance when she found herself in constant demand by her children. They were chronically bored and daily — no, hourly — wanted her to find interesting and exciting things for them to do. They were glued to the television, were demanding to go to rent video games, or were asking for playmates to be delivered for their entertainment. By the time her younger child turned three years of age, Linda decided that she would launch into a program of teaching the children how to entertain themselves, to become less dependent on her and more self-reliant.

TEACHING TOOLS

Teach children to use a positive inner voice. People "talk" to themselves all the time, and it's that inner voice that directs their feelings and behavior. When the inner voice is positive and self-affirming, it can increase a person's ability to rely on his own inner resources. Likewise, when things people say to themselves are negative ("This is awful!" "I'm an idiot, I can't do anything!"), their self-confidence can take a fatal nosedive. To help children improve their self-confidence and self-reliance, it is important to help their inner voice to be as self-affirming, positive, and "can do" in tone as possible.

Teachable Moment

"I'm so dumb!" Leslie said after she made a mistake on a crayon picture she had been drawing. "I make so many mistakes."

"How does making mistakes make you dumb?" Linda asked.

"I should be able to draw a dumb picture and not mess it up all the time," Leslie answered, pouting.

"How old are you?" Linda asked.

"Mom, you know I'm six . . . almost seven," Leslie answered, smiling.

"Well, it seems to me that if you're six, you should be able to make mistakes once in a while," Linda continued. "I make mistakes, and I'm a lot older than six."

"I don't like to make mistakes," Leslie answered.

"I don't think anybody likes to make mistakes, but we all still do. That's just the way humans are," Linda said. "I have a little voice inside my head that says it's okay to make mistakes, so I don't get upset with myself when I do."

"I have a little voice in my head that says I'm dumb," Leslie said. "How do I get the voice to say something else?"

"You just *make* it say something else," Linda answered. "When the voice says 'dumb,' you say out loud, 'I'm not dumb. I just made a mistake.' That way you will change the voice to say something healthier than 'dumb.' "

Over the next several weeks, Linda would hear Leslie talking out loud to herself as she tried to correct the little voice in her head. Linda also noticed that Leslie seemed somewhat happier and was even getting along better with her big brother. She seemed more self-reliant as she became less of a perfectionist in her own life.

Model self-entertainment. For your children to learn how to rely on themselves for entertainment, they need to be taught by example. Create a list of inexpensive, easily accessible activities that you enjoy, and choose to do one a day. The secret in your modeling is to describe how good it feels to be doing these activities, so your "audience" can connect your positive feelings with the activities.

"There is always something to do. Boredness stimulates unintelligence." —CLARE

Teachable Moment

"Mom, why aren't you watching TV? Your favorite shows are on tonight," Ben asked when he saw his mother pick up a book after dinner rather than turn on the television as she had generally done.

"I've decided I'm tired of TV, and I just want to read a good book instead," she answered. "Why don't you get a book and read, too?"

"I don't like to read; and besides, TV is more fun," Ben exclaimed as he picked up the TV remote control.

"No, Ben," Linda said firmly. "No TV tonight. We're going to entertain ourselves without any help from the Box."

"Mommy, I'm bored," Leslie whined. "I want to watch TV."

"You may get your crayons and draw for a while, play with your dolls, or play a game with Ben. You choose — either you find something to do around here to entertain yourself, or I can find a job for you to do to keep you busy. You decide what you want to do," Linda told her matter-of-factly.

After much grumbling and whining, the children did play a board game. This lesson was as enlightening for Linda as it was for her children because she had not realized how dependent her family was on her for entertainment, and how entrenched their family's dependency on television for entertainment had become. Moreover, the negative results — lack of energy, creativity, and resourcefulness — that were produced by this dependency were not apparent until she turned the TV off and began searching for truly nourishing ways to fulfill her nights and days.

Reduce television viewing time. Children, as well as many adults, can grow dependent on the entertainment offered by television. In order to reduce your children's dependence on

television and increase their self-reliance and ability to entertain themselves, their time spent viewing TV must be
restricted. To do this, meet with your children to draw up a
weekly viewing schedule of about one hour daily. Then
enforce the schedule, as you would any other house rule.

WARNING: DON'T ALLOW UNREGULATED TV.

Children who are allowed to watch whatever television
shows they want whenever they want to can become
dependent on being entertained by others in situations in
which they don't have to lift a finger to play. Such dependency is hard to overcome and, research has proven, can
lead to lowered reading scores and to childhood obesity.

Teachable Moment

"We're going to decide which TV shows we'll watch each
day, so let's make a list of the shows you like," Linda
announced one day.

"But why can't we watch anytime we want?" Leslie
demanded as her brother nodded in agreement.

"Because we watch too much, and it's not good for our
brains to be shut down for so long. We have also become
dependent on the TV characters to do our thinking — our
living — for us. We need to develop our own lives!" Linda
responded.

Her children grumbled about not wanting to think and
knowing that their lives could *never* be as cool as those
characters on TV.

"Now, what do you like to watch each day?" she asked
each of her children, continuing with her plan. When the
list was made, she asked each child to decide which he

or she liked best, then next best, and finally the least liked. From the ranking, she helped them pick an hour they could watch together, and Linda decided to defer her own viewing until after the children were in bed. She found that she ended up not even watching television and eventually discovered her children losing interest, as it became more fun to live outside of the living room couch than watching fictitious characters play in their make-believe homes.

Praise creativity. Children who learn to be creative will always be blessed with the inner tools to be self-entertaining. To learn creativity, children must be given the freedom to express their thoughts and feelings and must receive positive feedback for taking creative risk. Keep in mind that children who are given things like stickers and other tangible rewards for what they create eventually work only for the rewards rather than for the intrinsic reinforcement of the creative process.

Teachable Moment

"Look, Mommy!" Leslie demanded as she showed her mother a picture she had been working on.

"Oh, Leslie," Linda replied. "You must have worked very hard to make that picture. You must be very proud of yourself. Do you know what we might do? Let's use that picture to make a book that you can write yourself and then read anytime you want."

They began writing a story as Leslie told Linda what to put on the pages. Then Leslie illustrated the book and stapled it together.

"Can I take it to school and show my teacher?" Leslie

asked. Linda agreed, confident that the teacher would praise Leslie's effort rather than praise the pictures or the story. That way Leslie would continue to want to put forth creative effort rather than to expect to make something "wonderful" each time.

Teach self-reliance strategies. Children are often at a loss to know what to do when they're deprived of the passive entertainment — television — to which they are so accustomed. To help your children develop ways to entertain themselves, encourage them to think of safe, affordable, enjoyable activities that they can do by themselves and make lists of those activities. Then when they complain about there being nothing to do, ask them to consult their list. If they can't yet read, make the list for them and then read it to them. In order to encourage children to find alternative activities, praise them when they immerse themselves in one of these constructive activities, and offer to find work for them to do when they can't seem to find ways to entertain themselves on or off their list.

WARNING: DON'T ENTERTAIN CHILDREN CONSTANTLY.

Some parents are concerned that their children will be deprived if they aren't being entertained all the time. Parents who schedule days filled with activities are actually preventing their children from becoming self-reliant and developing experience in finding ways to entertain themselves. Allow free time during which children are required to find their own activities so that they can get practice in becoming self-entertaining.

Teachable Moment

"I'm bored," Ben said one Saturday. Linda knew that his best friend was away for the weekend, and the boys had planned to play in the clubhouse they had built in the backyard.

"I know you wanted to play with Lee today, but he's gone for the weekend," Linda responded. "What can you find to do that will be fun for you to do by yourself?"

"I don't know!" Ben answered angrily. "You won't let me watch TV, so I don't have anything to do."

"I think that you know of lots of things to do," Linda answered. "You have your list of things that you enjoy that we made together. If you want to keep from being bored, maybe you could find something on your list that would be fun to do today."

"I don't want to do those things! I wanted to play with Lee!" Ben retorted angrily.

"Well, Ben," Linda answered calmly, "I guess I'll have to find something for you to do. Let's see, you could vacuum for me, scrub the kitchen floor, or you could rake the leaves out of the flower beds. You decide what you want. You can find some way to entertain yourself or you can work for me."

Ben stomped off, and soon he was in the garage with a hammer, nailing boards together.

"What are you making?" Linda asked.

"I'm making a shelf for our clubhouse. When Lee sees it, he'll think it's really neat."

His mom smiled. "Ben, that's a great idea! You are so creative, and you entertain yourself so well," she said as she closed her eyes in grateful appreciation of the sign of resourcefulness that her son demonstrated. She knew that Ben *could* be resourceful, it just took her own self-discipline to keep from rescuing him from his boredom and providing the entertainment for him.

"Believe nothing, no matter where you read it, or who said it, no matter if I have said it, unless it agrees with your own reason and your own common sense."
— BUDDHA (6TH CENTURY B.C.)

1 5

SELF-MOTIVATION

"The purpose of life is a life of purpose."
— ROBERT BYRNE

mo·ti·vate *vb.* to provide with a motive
mo·tive *n.* **1.** something that causes a person to act **2.** moving
or tending to move to action **3.** of or relating to motion or the
causing of motion

○ "Mom, I have this big project to do, so I'm going to get
started on it now."

○ "I always do my homework before I play. That way I can
play without thinking about other stuff I have to do."

○ "I like the way my room looks when I keep it clean."

○ "I want to get up early Saturday so I can get my chores
done before baseball practice."

NAG, NAG, NAG! If you feel that all you do every day is
repeat, remind, and regret the behavior of your children, this
lesson is going to help you as much as your offspring. Imagine a set of chores, homework assignments, and taking care
of oneself as a brownie cake pan. When the bottom is up,
nothing warm and sweet and good can be created. But this

same pan, when turned right side up, can be used appropriately to produce a treat that is satisfying to that ever-hungry sweet tooth. So it is with self-motivation. But if *you* try to pour in the rules, nothing is produced. Let the children fill up their lives themselves.

To learn to fill themselves with motivation, children first have to develop an internalized control system. Such a system comes from living within a set of rules and boundaries which are initially established within a family. Children with an internalized set of rules are more likely to set goals for themselves, to respond to external structure in positive ways, and to respect themselves. Self-motivation is truly the foundation of self-reliance and independence, two goals that underlie healthy living in adulthood — the ultimate goal of both children and their parents.

"Make yourself the navigator as well as the pilot."
— WADE

WHAT DO WE MEAN BY SELF-MOTIVATED?

- To be self-motivated is to respond to internal forces that direct people toward their goals.
- To be self-motivated means that a person is able to respond to the intrinsic reinforcement of an activity rather than to always need extrinsic reinforcement.
- When a person is self-motivated, he has an almost automatic, self-driven internalized set of rules and boundaries.
- Being self-motivated is a sign of self-respect.

MEET THE WYZINSKI FAMILY

Wayne and Roberta Wyzinski were becoming concerned that their four children, eighteen-month-old Sally, five-year-old Daniel, seven-year-old Laura, and twelve-year-old Angela, seemed unable to do anything without being nagged and threatened. The older children's homework was never done without a battle, their rooms were a shambles, and their chores were not done unless a parent was standing over them at all times. Life in the Wyzinski household was not pleasant. Wayne and Roberta wanted so much for their children to be self-motivated, but knew that their constantly cracking the whip for them to accomplish what they considered important goals was not convincing their children of those goals' priority in their lives.

TEACHING TOOLS

Make and enforce house rules. In order for children to learn to motivate themselves, they need a set of rules that guide them in their daily living. Children who live in a world without clear rules tend to be impulsive and anxious because they lack guidance. Set rules for your children so that they understand what is expected of them. In developing rules for your children, state them in terms of what you want your children to *do* rather than what you *don't* want them to do. When rules are stated as *do* rules, children have a model of behavior that acts as a guiding principle. In addition, if the rules are made to be house rules, they are in force regardless of who the manager is at the time: parents, grandparents, baby-sitters, or friends.

Teachable Moment

"But why do I have to do that?" five-year-old Daniel whined.

"Because it's the rule," his mother replied calmly. "You

know that we met with you and your sisters last Sunday afternoon and made up a list of the rules that we need to follow in order to make our family run smoothly."

"But I don't want to always put my toys away when I'm done playing with them. I might want to use them again real soon," he wailed.

"I understand how you feel, but the rule says that you have to put them away after you are finished playing with them," Roberta answered, "and when you have put them away, you can then go do whatever you want to do."

"I'm not going to do it, and you can't make me!" he screamed.

Roberta was about to lose her cool, but she decided that she must take a stand and stick to her position regardless. "Let me tell you what the deal is here. When you have picked up the toys and put them away, then you can go on to do other things. I'm willing to wait for you to do what the rule says," and she patiently sat down next to him.

He yelled, struggled, and threatened, but she stood her ground. "You may go when you have followed the rule," she kept saying as calmly as she could. After a few minutes, he finally gave in and angrily put his toys away.

Roberta decided that, for now, she would ignore all the noise he was making. The important thing was to establish and enforce the rules, even if doing so was not popular. Over time, she knew it was a lesson that would result in her children being motivated to accomplish their goals instead of relying on her to nag them into it.

Help children set and accomplish reasonable goals. People who are self-motivated set both short- and long-term goals as well as understand the steps needed to accomplish what they set out to do. To help your children with reaching their objectives, it is important to assign tasks for children to do within the household and to help them with the steps needed to accomplish them. With young children (between two and six), simple chores such as putting napkins on the table, putting toys away, and putting dirty clothes in the hamper can be required; as children grow older (ages six through teens), more complex and time-consuming duties can be assigned such as cleaning up a room, washing windows, cleaning bathrooms, and raking leaves.

"I think I'm self-motivated because I want a good future, so I do things now without being asked, like doing my homework and taking out the trash." — JENNY

Teachable Moment

"Here is a list of chores for each of you to do every day," Roberta announced to her children. After the look of shock wore off their faces, the complaining began.

"I'll never get all this done," seven-year-old Laura wailed.

"It's not fair! Now we have to do everything around here," twelve-year-old Angela complained.

"Maybe we should plan how you can get all your chores done and still have time for your homework and for your playtime," Roberta suggested. "I'll get a pencil and some paper, and we can work out a schedule. I think we can get everything done and still have plenty of time."

Keeping a positive attitude was one secret of this family's ability to carry out their plan. Not only did they find that they had time to do everything they wanted, but they also had some "free" unscheduled time to use as they wanted; there was more time in the day because they were not wasting time complaining about being bored, or irritating each other with teasing, name-calling, and other put-downs.

Reward the process of work rather than the outcome. When children are materially rewarded for what they do, they learn to always expect those kinds of rewards. Rather than rewarding the *outcome* of a job well done, it is more important to reward the *process* required to reach the outcome. To help your children to become self-motivated, praise them for the work they do, rather than for the "great job" they have done.

WARNING: AVOID USING TANGIBLE REWARDS.

Children who are given things like stickers, toys, food, or money as rewards for what they accomplish learn to expect to be rewarded in these ways for their accomplishments. That makes them dependent on extrinsic rewards rather than on the intrinsic satisfaction of having done what they needed to do. In order to teach your children to motivate themselves, use praise for the actions they take to reach goals they have set, and avoid rewarding the reaching of the goal.

Teachable Moment

Five-year-old Daniel was busily working on a drawing, and Roberta didn't want to disturb him while he was being so industrious. Finally, he finished and presented his work for his mother's approval. She was tempted to tell him how beautiful his drawing was, but she caught herself.

"You really worked hard on this!" she exclaimed. "You

must be really proud of all the work you put into it!" She watched her son puff up with pride.

Later, when Laura and Angela finished their homework and presented it to Roberta, she again was tempted to praise what they had accomplished.

"You really worked hard today. You must feel good that you were able to accomplish so much and still have time to play before dinner," she said, conveying the strong message that the effort was what was being rewarded. Everyone can't succeed all the time, but effort is something that everyone must use to accomplish *any* goal.

Maintain a consistent world for children. Children who live in a consistent, predictable world will spend less time trying to figure out what will happen next, therefore giving them a more secure environment in which to be creative and come up with personal goals and dreams. In order for your children to be able to motivate themselves, it is important for you to maintain a neat and consistent household, for example. Keep eating and sleeping schedules as consistent as possible, and follow through with promises and plans — goals that take self-discipline for parents, too!

WARNING: AVOID NAGGING TO GET CHILDREN TO REACH THEIR GOALS.

Children won't learn to motivate themselves if they know that a parent or someone will nag them until they do what needs to be done. Nagging becomes a safety net that prevents children from taking on the responsibility they need to have to reach their goals. Instead of nagging, help children learn to motivate themselves by creating lists of goals and consequences for reaching or not reaching goals. Through the application of consequences, children learn to take on responsibility for reaching their own goals and making their own dreams come true.

"I think I am self-motivated because I get my homework done without being told." — NIKKI

Teachable Moment

Wayne and Roberta came to realize that their own behavior was important in helping their children learn self-motivation. They began to create a special time for dinner at least three times a week, realizing that sometimes they would need to be flexible enough to work around their children's sporting events.

"You said we could go to the mall on Saturday," Angela complained when her mother told her that she would have to stay home and do chores.

"Yes, I did say you could go with your friends for two hours on Saturday afternoon, but you also knew that you had chores to do and they had to be done before anything else could be done," Roberta reminded.

"But you *promised!*" Angela wailed. "You *never* keep your promises!"

"Remember the rules," Roberta answered calmly. "When you have done your chores, then you may do what you want to do. That's the way we do things in this family now."

"A promise is a promise," Angela continued to demand.

"But remember the rule," Roberta told her. "You have to do the things on your list before you have free time."

"Okay! Okay!" Angela shouted as she stomped off to her room. Roberta felt sorry that Angela was so angry, but she was proud of herself for sticking to the rules. She knew that she had to be consistent in order to help her children learn to follow through with their own steps to reach their goals.

Teach children to problem-solve. Problem-solving is a way for children to learn to think through problems and develop alternatives they could use to solve the problems. To teach your children to problem-solve, help them identify the nature of the problem; brainstorm potential solutions with them; and by looking at the consequences of each potential solution, help them choose the alternative that may best solve the problem.

WARNING: AVOID PROCRASTINATION.

Children who see adults do everything but meet their responsibilities only learn to procrastinate themselves as well. In order to help your children avoid this trap of procrastination, encourage yourself and your children to seize the moment. Thinking about what one "has to do" only makes the tasks seem more ominous and challenging.

Teachable Moment

"I have all this homework to do, and I don't think I can get it done before tomorrow," Angela wailed as she threw her backpack on the floor. "Our teacher is so mean! She gave us all this stuff to do for tomorrow!"

"That is a problem," Roberta responded with empathy. "What do you think you could do to get all this done?"

"I don't know!" Angela responded angrily. "I'll never get it all done."

"What do you think might help get this done?" Roberta continued.

Angela sat for a few minutes before answering. "I guess I could decide what's the most important thing to do first."

"That sounds like a good idea. How should you start?"

"Well, I guess I need to look at all the stuff I need to do. Let's see, I have some math problems to do and then I need to find some current events in the newspaper for social studies. Then I have to write ten sentences using our spelling words."

"What do you want to do first?" Roberta asked.

"I guess I'll get the math out of the way. Then I can do the spelling words. If I don't get it all done before dinner, I can go through the paper after dinner and find some current events."

"That sounds like a good plan. I'll keep Daniel and Sally out of your room so they won't disturb you while you work," Roberta answered.

Feeling good about taking control of her own home-work schedule, Angela could turn her mind over to the tasks at hand — and had all the work done before dinner — because she had a plan. Both Roberta and Wayne praised Angela at dinner for the great effort she had put into creating a plan and following through on it to get her homework done.

"Do every act of your life as if it were your last."
— MARCUS AURELIUS

16

RESPONSIBILITY

"I believe that every right implies a responsibility; every opportunity, an obligation; every possession, a duty." — JOHN D. ROCKEFELLER, JR.

re·spon·si·bil·i·ty *n.* 1. the state or fact of being responsible 2. an instance of being responsible 3. a particular burden of obligation upon a person who is responsible 4. something for which a person is responsible 5. reliability or dependability, especially in meeting debts or payments

- "You know I'll finish my homework because I *always* do it!"
- "I'll be responsible for taking care of my brother."
- "Trust me, Mom, I'll be home before dark."
- "Please, Mommy! I want it so bad! I promise I'll take care of my new coat."

"TAKE RESPONSIBILITY FOR YOUR words and actions," say parents who believe that by doing so, their children can be trusted by them . . . and by others. What are the steps in teaching this lesson? First, children have to be taught to move beyond thinking only about themselves and to see the greater good that engaging in responsible behavior can bring. Therefore, children need to learn to have empathy—

to be able to assume the role of others — in order to appreciate their feelings and to be sensitive to their needs. In the family, children who accept responsibility are essential in helping the family survive. They are seen as well behaved and helpful. In the larger social context, when each of us accepts responsibility for what he does, all of society works well. Teaching children responsibility is essential, therefore, to our family, to society, and to individual self-respect.

*"My parents always said that if you do the crime, you do the time." —*OLIVIA

WHAT DO WE MEAN BY RESPONSIBILITY?

- Learning responsibility means learning to behave so that one can be trusted.
- Taking responsibility means being helpful to the well-being of the family.
- Being responsible means being able to feel what others feel and to understand the needs of others.
- Responsibility refers to a way of responding with full knowledge that the consequences are one's own when tasks are done or not done.
- Taking responsibility for one's actions means thinking about their outcomes and impact before saying or doing things.
- Responsible people have the ability to defer gratification when needed.

MEET THE WU FAMILY

Charles and Claire Wu wanted their boys to behave in responsible ways, particularly when they were in public.

Eight-year-old Kyle and five-year-old Nathan, however, had ideas of their own. They seemed totally into themselves; what they wanted was more important than the needs of anyone else. Chuck and Claire wanted to teach their sons responsibility, because they were tired of the demands of these two tyrants, the constant need to pick up after them, and their own disgusting habit of nagging them about their rarely met responsibilities. At this rate, the boys would never be able to hold down a job, let alone be successful in school, if they didn't begin to take responsibility for what they said or did.

TEACHING TOOLS

Model responsibility. Because responsibility refers to a *way* of approaching tasks to be done, it is an abstract concept that may be difficult for young children to learn. Therefore, it is important to show children, as often as possible, examples of responsible behavior. When you model responsibility to your children, describe what you are doing, and make a connection between the benefits of responsible behavior and the well-being of the family.

Teachable Moment

"Why can't we go to the video store and rent some new games?" Kyle demanded.

His brother echoed, "Yeah, why?"

"Because I need to get things done in the kitchen so we can eat dinner when your dad gets home," Claire answered.

"Dad can wait for dinner!" Kyle replied. "I'm bored with the games we have; I want to get something new now!"

"It wouldn't be right to make him wait," their mom explained. "He's had a long day, and we need to have dinner ready when he gets here. I have my responsibilities and your dad has his. Tonight, I'm responsible for fixing dinner on time; and today, your dad was responsible for earning money for us to have. We all have to take care of our responsibilities or the family will suffer."

"But we need a new game!" Nathan chimed in, oblivious of the rest of the family's concerns.

Claire realized that the concept she was trying to convey was getting lost. "Imagine that you are Dad, and you have just come home from the office after eight hours of work," she described. "You're looking forward to a hot meal and an update of all of the day's events. How do you feel when you come home and no one's here?"

Nate was quiet for a moment. Then he protested, "But I want to get a video now — I don't want to eat now."

"How about we compromise?" his mother suggested. "When we have eaten dinner and all cleaned the dishes, that will mean that we have taken care of those responsibilities. You'll be in charge of doing what you need to do around here from about four P.M. to seven. Then we can go to the video store, if you choose."

"Okay, Mom," Kyle agreed, and his brother chimed in his agreement as well.

Claire was glad that Kyle and Nathan at least knew that taking responsibility for something often required some sacrifice. She guessed that they would eventually understand the broader meaning of duty and responsibility. But for now, they needed to experience the rewards of carrying out their responsibilities and seeing how important they were to the well-being of their family.

Use lists to remind children of their responsibilities. In order for children to remember their household chores, parents often have to remind them. However, those frequent reminders make children dependent on parents for their motivation and the assurance that they will carry out their duties. In order to teach children to take responsibility for their jobs, give them lists of chores that they can follow, and make access to their privileges dependent on completing the duties.

WARNING: DON'T USE TANGIBLE REINFORCEMENT.

Children who are given stickers and other tangible rewards for doing things for which they are responsible learn to expect a material gift every time they follow directions or act responsibly. To avoid this trap of tangible rewards, make having privileges contingent on doing those things for which they are responsible. By using Grandma's Rule — when you have done what you have to do, then you may do what you want to do — children learn to do those things for which they are responsible before they play.

Teachable Moment

"How many times do I have to tell you boys to do your chores?" Claire heard herself say on Saturday morning as Kyle and Nathan absorbed their weekly fix of television cartoons.

"We'll do them later, Mom," Kyle answered. Nathan sat in a trance as he stared unblinking at the set.

"Later! Later! That's all I hear. Well, later doesn't cut it. You'll do it now!" Claire shouted as she turned off the TV.

Feeling worse than she had before her outburst, Claire

realized that yelling at her boys had only created conflict, not taught them responsibility. She and Chuck devised a plan to solve the problem, both of them feeling sure that it would teach responsibility, yet both of them knowing that it would require lots of self-discipline on their parts, too. That very afternoon, they outlined their plan with their boys.

"We have made lists of chores you have to do each day, and those to do on the weekend," Claire began. "When you finish a chore, just check it off the list, and when the list is done, you may do what you want to do."

"You mean we can't watch TV until our chores are done?" Kyle asked, unbelieving.

"You got it!" Chuck answered. "Kyle, it's not as if the list is long. All you have to do is to make your bed each day, put your dirty clothes in the hamper, hang up your towel after you shower, and make sure the dog has food in his dish. That's not so much. I know you can handle it."

"Yeah, but . . ." Nathan began. "How am I going to remember to do everything? I can't remember all that."

"That's why we made you lists," Claire answered. "That way you can always check your list to see if you have anything you need to do. And we won't nag you or remind you. It's your responsibility."

Each day, Chuck and Claire checked the lists and the quality of the work done. Taking into account the boys' ages and ability levels, the Wus weren't too demanding in their control of quality. But from time to time, the job didn't measure up; then that "worker" was required to redo it. That happened with Nathan's bed-making one day.

"You really did a good job pulling the sheet up tight," Claire told Nathan. "Now, when the pillow is put where it belongs and the blanket is pulled up so that it's even along the side, your bed will be made really well."

By praising what was done right, Claire didn't discount her son's effort, and by pointing out what could improve the job, she left no mystery about what needed to be done. The combination of job lists, feedback about job performance, and specific ways of correcting problems reduced parental nagging and dramatically improved job performance in the Wu household.

Reward responsibility. Another way for children to learn to identify responsible behavior is to praise it when it occurs. When your children show responsibility, describe the behavior to them and tell them that what they're doing is appreciated.

Teachable Moment

When Chuck saw Nathan ride his bike up to the garage, open the door, and park it in its proper place in the garage, he was amazed and pleased.

"Nate, buddy," he began. "You put your bike away. That was very responsible of you. That means that it won't get wet if it rains, run over by the car, or stolen. That means we won't have to replace it, and that's good for our family."

Nathan looked puzzled but liked his dad's attention.

Later that day, Chuck commented on Kyle's remembering to turn off the kitchen light. "Kyle, that was so responsible of you to remember to turn off the kitchen light. It saves electricity . . ." and before he could finish, Kyle said, "Yeah, I know. If we don't waste electricity, we don't use so much fossil fuel, and it saves the environment. We learned that in science."

"Well, it looks like you know a lot about saving the

environment. If we all take as much responsibility for the environment as you do, we'll have this old planet around for a long time to come," Chuck said as he gave his son a little hug.

Later that week as Claire was cruising through the house before leaving to drop the boys off at school before going on to work, she passed Kyle's room and saw that he was making his bed.

"Kyle, how nice that you're making your bed before we have to leave," she said. "That is so responsible of you."

"I want to do all my chores on my list so I can play when I get home," he answered in his matter-of-fact way.

Out of the corner of her eye, she saw Nathan hurry back to his room, and when she went to check on him, he, too, was making his bed.

"Why, Nathan," she said, "you're making your bed, too."

"Yeah, I'm responsible," he answered. "I do what I'm supposed to."

Stifling her desire to laugh at his overestimation of his sense of responsibility, she simply thanked him for doing his chores. She knew that her praise of bed-making would keep that behavior in play at least for a few more days! Remembering to praise their boys' behavior was not always easy for Charles and Claire, but they could see their efforts paying off as Nathan and Kyle continued to assume responsibility for their chores.

Make sure homework is done. Often children avoid the responsibility of doing homework by denying that they have any to do. If your children are not carrying out their homework responsibilities, make sure you know what the assignments are, and make a rule that a child's homework is done before his evening privileges begin.

WARNING: DON'T RESCUE CHILDREN FROM THE CONSE-QUENCES OF THEIR BEHAVIOR.

Children who are learning responsibility need to understand that they might suffer the consequences if they don't assume responsibility for their behavior. If parents rescue children from the consequences of their own behavior, then they won't learn that the positive consequences of taking responsibility for what one has said or done outweigh the negative ones of shirking them.

Teachable Moment

"Do you have any homework, Kyle?" Claire would ask every day after school, and Kyle would always answer that he did not. But when report cards came home, his teacher generally noted that he didn't always turn in his homework. So Chuck and Claire decided to begin a program that Chuck referred to at his office as "management by objectives complete with performance appraisal." To the boys, he just called it a "new program."

"Kyle, this is how the new program will work," Chuck explained. "Every day, you'll write your assignments in this notebook, get your teacher to sign here that you have the assignment right, and bring the book home with your homework. You need to do the homework before you get to play or do anything you want."

"What happens if I forget and go outside first?" Kyle asked, concerned.

"Well, then you'll spend the whole evening in your

study hall at the dining room table," Chuck answered matter-of-factly. "So you choose. Which outcome do you want: Do homework for thirty minutes and then go play all evening, or play for thirty minutes and then have to spend the whole night in study hall?"

Kyle could easily see which choice was the most beneficial to his agenda of wanting to play basketball as much as possible. He chose to follow the rule, and was rewarded by accepting the least objectionable consequence.

"Nothing we do ever stands by itself. If it is good, it will serve some good purpose in the future. If it is evil, it may haunt us and handicap our efforts in unimagined ways." — ELEANOR ROOSEVELT

17

HONESTY

"Living the truth in your heart without compromise brings kindness into the world. Attempts at kindness that compromise your heart cause only sadness." — 18TH-CENTURY MONK

honest *adj.* **1.** truthful; trustworthy **2.** sincere or genuine **3.** gained by fair means **4.** frank; open

- "I can't let you help me with my homework. That wouldn't be honest."

- "Mom, didn't that lady give you too much change? We shouldn't keep it."

- "I broke the lamp in the living room playing with my football after you told me not to. I'm sorry."

- "I like her because she's sincere. I always know where I stand."

"HONESTY IS THE BEST policy" is an old adage that children today may find challenged in every newscast they watch, every newspaper they read. When once it may have been considered a rule broken by only the most incorrigible, examples of dishonesty are of almost epidemic proportions all around us. Cheating on tests, lying to reporters, stealing money from the government — from these unethical examples, children are not going to learn the benefits that being honest provides to one's sense of strong character and moral fiber.

Who are the world's best teachers of honesty? Family and peers are keys to this lesson-building, and are providing those lessons with every decision they support, every example they model of living life honestly and compassionately. In order to learn honesty, children must care about disappointing their parents and others, care about what others think of them, and care about their own self-image. This caring voice inside tells them subconsciously, "I want to be known as an honest person!" As a wise teacher once wryly remarked, "If I never tell a lie, I don't have to remember anything I've said."

"If you tell a lie, it just keeps going and going. Learn to tell the truth, then the lie will stop." — AUDREY

WHAT DO WE MEAN BY HONESTY?

- Honesty means the ability to be trusted by others.
- Caring enough to want to do the right thing is a sign of an honest person.
- An honest person cares about the rights of others and does not take advantage of them.
- To be respectable, have a good reputation, and have honorable principles are all important to honest people.
- Honest people are truthful in sharing their thoughts and feelings.

MEET THE CARLTON FAMILY

Samantha and Les Carlton were interested in raising their children, Lucy, aged three, and Jonathan, aged eight, to be honest, upright citizens. But frequently, the children weren't as honest as their parents would have liked them to be. Jonathan would lie about whether or not he had homework, and Lucy was notorious for taking her brother's things without asking. After a particularly bad week of rampant dishonesty, the Carltons decided it was time to begin to teach their children the benefits of caring about others (and oneself) enough to act honestly in their exchanges with others. When the children lied, Samantha and Les knew their offspring were hurting themselves as well as the victims of their dishonesty. The task at hand was how to teach this lesson to their children so they could trust that what they did and said was the truth.

TEACHING TOOLS

Model honesty. As the winds of right and wrong waft children's moral decision-making hither and yon, it is difficult to expect children to always be honest. Evaluate your own behavior and hold steadfast to being a model of honesty — even when you're tempted at the moment to take an easier path than telling the truth seems to be. As you drive, obey speed limits; on the telephone, give honest answers to those who called your number mistakenly; when given incorrect change, remind the clerk. It's these daily examples that make a lasting impression.

Teachable Moment

As is often the case with busy people, the Carltons were running late and were in a hurry to get to the party. Les was driving somewhat above the speed limit when the ever-helpful Lucy called it to his attention. "Daddy, too fast!"

Jonathan immediately chimed in, "Never mind, Dad, I'll watch out for police cars."

"No, Jon. Lucy's right. I shouldn't be driving so fast," their dad admitted. "It's not only against the law to be driving above the speed limit, but it's dangerous. The speed limit is supposed to protect people from driving too fast and making it dangerous for everybody else. I'll slow down. Next time we should leave earlier so we'll have plenty of time and not be in such a hurry."

Les realized that he wanted to be a walking role model of honesty for his children, a task that could cause him to serve a dual purpose — force him to evaluate *and* change some of his behaviors, too.

Reward honesty in your children. As preschoolers, children are generally honest because they don't understand dishonesty. Verbally rewarding children's honesty early and immediately can support and encourage it. When you see honesty in your children, praise them for being honest by describing what they are doing and how much their honesty means to those around them.

Teachable Moment

Samantha always asked Jonathan about his homework when he arrived home from school. She knew he would rather be playing with his friends after school than be doing homework, and if she didn't ask, he wouldn't tell her about what he had to do.

That's why she was so surprised when he came in after school and said, "I have to finish my math worksheet and then study for the spelling test. I'll finish my math while I have my snack. Then can we study the spelling words after dinner, so I can play now until dark?"

"Jon, that was very honest of you to tell me about your homework," his mom said with a big smile and pat on the back for Jon. "Because you were honest with me, I'll be happy to work with you after dinner on your spelling." Samantha could tell that Jon was pleased that she was pleased, making his decision a win-win one for everyone.

Teach children to be honest with themselves. Sometimes children have difficulty taking responsibility for their actions. In order to help them be honest about who is responsible for their behavior, it is important to help them understand cause-and-effect relationships and to learn alternative ways of behaving when they make mistakes. Such teaching involves helping children sometimes feel some guilt, a force that may result when children feel what another person feels.

Teachable Moment

When Samantha entered the kitchen, she saw Lucy standing over a puddle of juice on the kitchen floor. "What happened?" she asked.

"Jon made me dop juice!" Lucy exclaimed loudly.

"I did not!" Jon shrieked. "I was sitting here eating my breakfast and minding my own business."

"You looked at me! Dat made me dop my juice! You did it! You clean up mess!" Lucy yelled at him.

"Lucy, I'm sure Jon feels bad that you are accusing him of something he didn't do," her mother calmly explained, using "feeling" language. "He was sitting at the table. He couldn't have made you drop the juice. It's not honest to blame him for a mistake you made. Here, I'll help you clean it up."

It is helpful to confront children with the fact that

saying "I did it" gains more support and care from others than dishonest blaming. Being honest with themselves and swallowing the consequences of doing so are doses of reality children need to take on a daily basis to understand how to cope when life hands them little — or big — spills.

"Being honest is one of the most important values because if no one trusts you, no one will like you."
—JOE

Teach children to problem-solve situations. When children have difficulty being honest when faced with challenges, part of the solution is to help them learn problem-solving. When children can problem-solve, they are less likely to lie in order to make themselves look better in the eyes of those they want to impress, to get out of doing something that they didn't want to do in the first place, or to avoid punishment. By problem-solving, they take more control over their choices, thereby being able to feel better about which they select. To teach the virtue of honesty, first help your child understand the nature of the problem. Then encourage him to brainstorm possible solutions to the problem and evaluate the potential outcome of each solution before selecting the one that might yield the best outcome.

WARNING: DON'T USE HARSH OR CORPORAL PUNISHMENT WHEN CHILDREN ARE DISHONEST.

Children who are punished harshly for any reason lose respect for the punisher and only learn to avoid that person rather than to avoid the behavior that resulted in the punishment.

Teachable Moment

After Lucy and her mom cleaned up the juice that Lucy had spilled, her mom tried to help Lucy assume the responsibility for the event in a calm, helpful way. She decided to problem-solve with other ways that the little mishap could have been handled. "Lucy, when you spill something, what do you think you can do about that problem?"

"I don't know. I could come get you!" Lucy answered brightly.

"That's an interesting possibility. How do you suppose that would turn out?"

"Maybe you'd get mad," Lucy said with a worried brow.

"Well, if you're afraid that might happen, what else could you do?"

"I get paper stuff and clean it up myself!" Lucy smiled proudly.

"And if you did that, how do you suppose that would turn out?"

"Well, you'd like that, Mommy, if I cleaned my messes!" she excitedly noted.

"Is that the solution to this problem that you would like best? Let's try it to see if it would work out for you," her mom concluded.

In teaching problem-solving, Samantha helped Lucy become more self-sufficient as well as assume responsibility for her own behavior. Even at her tender preschool age, she knew right from wrong when given the opportunity to choose between the two in an environment that was caring, not critical.

Look for honesty in others. When children see honesty modeled in other people whom they respect, they are encouraged to be honest, too. Point out honest acts when you can, including how the honest person felt, so that children can see that honesty is the best policy because it provides positive rewards. In addition, share how dishonest persons in the news, for example, always pay a heavy price for their hurtful behavior. By contrasting the benefits of honesty with the damage of dishonesty, children can feel how much better life is when honesty becomes part of their behavior repertoire.

Teachable Moment

While the Carlton family was shopping one day, they witnessed a person who had been given too much change by a clerk. The clerk was very appreciative and said that she would have had to pay back the money herself if the customer had not been so honest.

"Wasn't that nice that the customer gave the clerk the change back when she was given too much?" Samantha began, looking her children squarely in the eye. "It is so nice that there are still honest people in the world! What would you have done if the clerk had given you more change than you were entitled to?"

This event led to a good discussion about character and integrity — two words that the children didn't actually understand but were working on building, with their parents' help.

Demonstrate the harm dishonesty can do. To show children that dishonesty doesn't pay, take any opportunity possible to talk about the negative effects of dishonesty. While watching television, talk about the consequences of dishonesty in the roles of the characters; when discussing the events of the day, take the opportunity to point out consequences of dishonesty at work, and how much time and energy it took for a colleague to apologize for his lie and make up for his wrongdoing by having to work overtime to correct his mistakes.

"My parents always told me it is better to tell the truth about something and not get in as much trouble than it is to lie about something and have your parents find out the truth on their own later and get in more trouble." — SHAUNA

Teachable Moment

"Jonathan, did you clean your room?" Les asked his son. "It needs to be done before we leave for your ball game."

"It's clean," Jonathan lied. He didn't want to take the time now, and besides, he was too excited about his upcoming baseball game and the prospect of playing first base. He couldn't keep his mind on room cleaning.

At the ball field, Jonathan took his place on first base and carefully watched the play. The game was slow, so he had time to think about the fact that he had lied to his dad, and he would undoubtedly get caught in his lie when he got home. The more he thought about it, the more it weighed on his mind, and when he looked at the stands and saw his parents sitting there, he really felt guilty. After he missed two throws and failed to tag a runner at first base, his coach replaced him and sent him to right field.

"Dad, I need to tell you something," Jonathan commented as they began to drive home after the game.

"What is it, buddy?" Les answered.

"I didn't really clean my room before we left," Jonathan said sheepishly. "I'm sorry."

"I'm sorry, too," Les answered seriously. "I thought I could trust you to tell me the truth, no matter what."

Later that afternoon, Jonathan and Les were sitting on the bed looking at the now clean room. "I guess you've felt pretty bad about what happened today," Les began. "And I'll bet that's why you missed those throws to first. You usually don't let those go by like that. You probably felt pretty guilty."

"Yeah, I did," Jonathan replied quietly. "I didn't like how I felt, and I thought about it a lot." He was quiet for a bit and then said, "Ricky asked me if I could sleep over at his house tonight. Can I?"

"I'm sorry," Les answered. "I wish you could. But because of your dishonesty today, I don't think it would be right."

Les really felt bad about denying his son's request, but he knew that by experiencing the unpleasant outcome of lying, his son would understand the cost of doing so and learn that the price of honesty seems a reasonable one to pay.

Watch out for those "little white lies."   Children are natural imitators and will copy the behavior of those whom they most respect. Take care to avoid any and all shapes and sizes of lying; your child will be watching your actions that always speak louder than words!

"Being honest has been a part of all my life because my parents think lies make life confusing." —SAMANTHA

Teachable Moment

Jon answered the telephone and heard the voice of a neighbor he knew his mother didn't like and didn't want to talk to. "Tell her I'm not here," his mom said, agitated. "No! She'll know that's not the truth. You'd never say I'm not here to a stranger. Tell her I'm taking a shower."

"Mom, I don't want to lie to Mrs. Adams. Please, just talk to her," Jon agonized.

"Go ahead and tell her what I said!" his mom retorted, becoming even more upset as she found herself instructing her child to lie.

Modeling dishonesty in any form and encouraging children to lie not only teaches lying but confuses children, who need more concrete, consistent rules to follow. Samantha decided that it was only hurting herself (and her neighbor and the children) to lie about her whereabouts; besides, it just wasn't something she felt comfortable doing. She apologized to her children, explaining that she had been wrong to handle the situation by lying. Problem-solving what she could do next time helped her realize that one is never too old to learn lessons of honesty.

"We should stop kidding ourselves. We should let go of things that aren't true. It's always better with the truth." —R. BUCKMINSTER FULLER

18

TRUSTWORTHINESS

"What you deny others will be denied to you, for the plain reason that you are always legislating for yourself; all your words and actions define the world you want to live in." — THADDEUS GOLAS

> **trust** *n.* **1. a.** assured reliance on the character, ability, strength, or truth of someone or on something **b.** one in which confidence is placed **2.** dependence on something future or contingent **3.** a charge or duty imposed in faith or confidence or as a condition of some relationship

- "I know I can depend on you to do what I've asked you to do."

- "Mom, you can depend on me. I'll get my chores done before I leave."

- "I know I can trust you to behave yourself when you spend the weekend with Blake."

- "Trust me! You know I'll pay you back."

"LEAN ON ME" IS a famous song made popular for its haunting melody and honest lyrics. "Everybody needs a body to lean on," a popular line from a Bob Dylan lyric, reminds us of the importance of being dependable as well. Why all this fuss about being trustworthy? This trait of being able to be "leaned on," trusted, and depended on is a precious one that can become a part of a child's behavior pattern at an early age. In order to learn to be trustworthy, it is important to teach children to care about themselves as well as about others.

We all know "Rocks of Gibraltar," people who are tough in times of a crisis. Even as toddlers, they listen to parents' woes and genuinely care about making their "owies" better. These qualities are teachable as part of lessons in caring about oneself, not just about others. When one cares about oneself and one's fellow humans, one makes sure that promises are kept, trust is developed, and the goal of being dependable is met. The nifty part of meeting this goal is its reflex action: When others depend on you because you're trustworthy, they are likely to return the favor.

"When somebody can put their trust in you, you should feel honored." — KRISTINA

WHAT DO WE MEAN BY TRUSTWORTHINESS?

- A trustworthy person cares about the needs of others.
- The desire to behave in such a way that people will trust you is strong in dependable people.
- To be trustworthy, one must have sufficient self-respect that the opinions of others count.
- Those who make the maximum effort to keep their promises are able to develop a reputation for being trustworthy.

MEET THE SILVERMAN FAMILY

Aaron and Phyllis Silverman wanted their daughters, ten-year-old Rebecca and six-year-old Rachel, to learn how to be trustworthy before they reached their teens. They had a long road ahead of them, they feared, because Rebecca would sometimes lie about whether or not she had finished her homework before watching television or going out to play, and Rachel just stuffed her clean wash in the closet instead of putting it away. In order for their daughters to earn their parents' trust, Aaron and Phyllis decided to make a concerted effort to teach them the skills that would lead each of them down the road of becoming someone they could count on to tell the truth and to do what they said they would do.

TEACHING TOOLS

Model dependability. Children learn best when they see others do things that they are required to do. In order to teach your children the skills of being trustworthy, it is important to show them on a daily basis how adults can be dependable. Try to keep promises made, be on time, carry out threats, and follow through with plans you make, unless you have an honest reason for changing them. In addition, choose the words you use to describe possible plans with caution. If you *think* that you *might* go to the movie on Saturday night with the children, tell them so, using these three words, "I will try," instead of saying, "I promise we will go to the movies Saturday."

Teachable Moment

"But you promised to take us to the movies today!" Rachel whined. "You never keep your promises!"

"In the first place, I didn't promise to take you to the movies today. I said we would try to go if we could. But you know that Rebecca has a soccer game this afternoon, and we are going to the game with her," Phyllis explained calmly. "And in the second place, I do try to keep my promises, and I'm careful to tell you when something is a promise. So when I say we might be able to do something, please ask me if it's a promise."

"Okay, Mom. But I still want to go to the movies sometime," Rachel said. "Can we go next Saturday?"

"I'm not sure. We'll have to see what the schedule looks like. But if there isn't anything else going on, we can go."

"You promise?" Rachel immediately asked.

"All I can promise is that we can look at the schedule and plan to go if nothing else is going on," Phyllis said patiently. "I can't promise that we'll go until we know whether or not we'll have time."

Phyllis was pleased that her daughter was learning the difference between a "possibility" and a "promise" — an important distinction she would need to make her whole life long.

Demand that children keep promises. Children often make promises that they can't keep. Helping them to moderate their promises and to follow through with them once they have made them are steps to their developing the virtue of being trustworthy.

WARNING: DON'T NAG CHILDREN.

Children who are nagged by their parents to always do what they say they are going to do fail to learn how to become dependable, because they know that if they don't do what they are expected to do, someone will remind them to. Moreover, it is usually easier to endure the unpleasantness of being nagged to having to take responsibility for one's own words and actions.

So teach this virtue without becoming the scapegoat: Use lists as reminders of what needs to be done, and make accomplishing the tasks on the list the prerequisite for getting to do what your child wants to do. By using Grandma's Rule — when you have done what you have to do, then you may do what you want to do — children learn that their free time is dependent on completing their chores.

Teachable Moment

"I'll get my homework done before it's time to go to the program. I can do it, I promise. I'll just watch the rest of this show, and then I'll get started," Rebecca promised her mother.

Phyllis knew that Rebecca had a lot of homework to finish before her school concert at seven. She would need every bit of time she had if she was going to get it finished before they left.

"How much do you have to do?" she asked innocently.

"Not much. I'll get it finished. No sweat!" came the answer.

"What exactly do you have to do?" Phyllis pursued the truth from her daughter.

"Well, I have forty math problems, some English sentences to write, some vocabulary words to learn, and then I have to write a hundred words about the rain forest we've been studying in science."

"Wow!" Phyllis exclaimed. "That sounds like a lot. Are you sure you can get it all done? How long do you think it'll take to do the math problems?"

"Not long. About forty-five minutes, I guess. That's how

long it took to do yesterday's assignment." Becky was now frowning. She looked at the clock and made some mental calculations. "Maybe I'd better get started," she continued soberly as she turned off the TV and headed for her room.

"I think you've made a sensible decision. I'd hate for you to not be able to keep the promise you made about finishing before the program. It's very important that we keep our promises," Phyllis said as she walked with Becky to her room. "I'll call you when dinner is ready."

Establish home duties. Children who have responsibilities to fulfill at home learn dependability as they are counted on to carry out their duties. The difficulty most parents face, however, is getting children to actually do their chores. To motivate your children to do the things they've been assigned to do, make lists for them to follow and allow them to have privileges, such as playing with friends or watching television, only after the list has been completed. By learning this work ethic, children learn to do what they have to do before they do what they want to do, the core of trustworthiness.

WARNING: DON'T ALLOW CHILDREN TO PROCRASTINATE.

Children who are allowed to put off difficult (or simple!) chores fail to learn to be trustworthy, because they can't set priorities. Rather than letting children do what they want to do before they do what they have to do, invoke Grandma's Rule. When they learn to do the hard things first, they won't have any reason to procrastinate.

Teachable Moment

"I want to go to Molly's on Saturday," Rebecca announced when she came home from school. "Can I?"

"Yes you may, when you have done your chores and cleaned your room," Phyllis answered.

"But I want to go before I do that junk!" Becky complained. "I'll do my chores after I get back. I promise."

"I know you'd like to go early in the day, but you know the rule," Phyllis reminded. "Everything on your list has to be done before you can do anything else."

"It's not fair. Nobody else has to do things before they get to play. I hate this place!" she exclaimed, stomping her feet all the way outside.

On Saturday, however, Becky was up early finishing cleaning her room, which she had started straightening up the night before. After she vacuumed the carpets and cleaned the bathroom she shared with her sister, she cleaned herself up and was ready to go.

"You must really feel proud of yourself for doing all your work so fast and so well. Now you can go to your friend's, and I'll be glad to take you," Aaron told his daughter as she turned in her checklist of chores all finished. "Becky, I feel so good that I can depend on you."

"My parents said, 'If we cannot depend on you, then how can others depend on you?' " — DAN

Reinforce trusting acts. Children can act dependably quite often, and it is the duty of parents to praise their being trustworthy when it happens. Offering the gift of verbal praise when children act dependably accomplishes several goals: It teaches children the behaviors that are important; it makes children feel good about themselves and their accomplishments; and it increases the probability that the behavior will be repeated. To help your children absorb the virtue of being trustworthy, watch for dependable acts. When you see them, point them out to your children by describing the behavior.

WARNING: DON'T USE TANGIBLE REWARDS.

Children who are given stickers, candy, toys, or any other tangible rewards for doing things they are required to do fail to incorporate being trustworthy as an internally motivated way of behaving. Instead, they come to expect to get something (material) for everything they do; without rewards, they figure that there is no reason for them to do what's expected of them.

Rather than give material rewards, let your children earn their privileges by completing their duties. Using Grandma's Rule teaches children that they must do what's required before doing what they want.

Teachable Moment

Rachel finished her breakfast and climbed down from the table. She turned, took her cereal bowl from the table, and carried it to the sink. She then pulled over a step stool, climbed up, rinsed her bowl out, and put it in the dishwasher. Finally, she took a sponge and wiped her place at the table. After she put the cereal away, she skipped off to play.

Phyllis went into the kitchen after her daughter had left it sparkling clean and marveled at how Rachel had left it so tidy. Grinning from ear to ear, she found Rachel playing upstairs with her favorite doll and lavished her behavior with praise.

"Rachel, you did such a nice job cleaning up after breakfast. You even remembered to put the cereal away.

I'm so pleased that I can depend on you to clean up after yourself," Phyllis beamed, and Rachel smiled proudly.

Phyllis noted that all day, Rachel took care of her duties without being asked, and she even volunteered to help when she really didn't need to. That was proof positive that Rachel was following her own set of expectations for how she wanted to act, which pleased her mother as much as the virtuous behavior itself.

"There is joy in transcending self to serve others."
— MOTHER TERESA

19

SELF-DISCIPLINE

"Self-reverence, self-knowledge, self-control,
These three alone lead life to sovereign power."
—ALFRED, LORD TENNYSON

self-dis·ci·pline *n.* 1. self-control 2. discipline and training of oneself, usually for improvement

- "Yes, I understand the rule, and I'm sorry I broke it."

- "I remembered the rule and decided not to hit my brother."

- "Mommy, what's the rule about toys?"

- "I like playing here because there are rules."

SELF-DISCIPLINE, AS DISPLAYED BY the children in the above comments, is not a term people use in everyday parenting. But it should be, because it is at the heart of the ability to lead a self-reliant, self-sufficient life. It also takes self-discipline to make choices that may mean less playing around (fun) immediately, but a greater sense of accomplishment (satisfaction) later. In fact, "fun" versus "satisfaction" is often the dilemma children face regarding their behavior in school, sports, and social situations. But when armed with self-discipline, a child can confidently choose satisfying activities, such as doing homework, rather than a "fun" shortcut, such as copying someone else's work. "It's better in the long run" and "You'll appreciate this one day" are two maxims that lose their impact on children who cannot fathom anything farther than today. But teaching self-discipline as a daily skill will serve children well today as well as "in the long run."

WHAT DO WE MEAN BY SELF-DISCIPLINE?

- Behaving from an internal frame of reference rather than from external control of an authority figure — parent, teacher, or baby-sitter, for example — demonstrates self-discipline.
- A self-disciplined person is able to understand and project himself into another person's "world."
- Making up one's own mind about the boundaries for behavior and respecting the boundaries of others are signs of self-discipline.
- Being able to forgo one's own pleasure and immediate gratification for the greater good takes self-discipline.
- Setting goals and working toward them is a key ingredient in self-discipline.
- Self-discipline is a necessary tool in unlocking the key elements of good character.

MEET THE MARCO FAMILY

Jill Marco and her husband, Tony, were observing how loud, destructive, and truly oppositional their sons, three-year-old Bobby and five-year-old Carl, were when playing together. Giving them freedom to explore and not setting many limits on their behavior would allow them to grow up to be adults who would be secure and creative, their parents surmised. But just the opposite was happening!

Unsure of how to proceed, Jill and Tony did an about-

face. They demanded that their children behave appropriately and spanked them when the boys weren't behaving
by adult standards. The results of this experiment were
disastrous, too. This parenting style only created more chaos,
anger, and rebellion.

It was then that Jill and Tony decided to try to teach their
children a set of internal controls for their behavior instead
of being "controlled" by their parents. *Voilà!* The results this
time were a parent's dream come true: The more the children learned about making choices and accepting the
consequences of them, the more appropriate and self-
disciplined their behavior became.

*"It really helps to be self-disciplined, because you
are much more independent and organized."* — KATIE

TEACHING TOOLS

Set rules — limits and boundaries. Children need rules for
several reasons: to help govern their behavior, to develop an
internal system of organization, and to be able to predict
how life's events will turn out. Set rules for your children's
behavior by deciding what you want them to *do* rather than
what you *don't* want them to do. "Do" rules remind children
of the goals you have set for their behavior and describe new
behaviors you want them to acquire. "Don't" rules only tell
children what they are not supposed to do; they don't focus
on new, parent-approved options to replace them.

Teachable Moment

"Things are getting out of control around here," Jill said to
Tony one evening after the boys had gone to bed. "It

seems like I spend all my time nagging the boys to get them to do anything."

"Don't have much self-discipline, do they?" Tony answered as he flipped the channels on the TV.

"We need some rules," Jill continued. "It seems like they don't have any order to their lives, and rules might give them some direction."

"What kind of rules?" Tony asked absently.

"You know, rules about chores and about getting along with each other and stuff like that," Jill answered.

After more discussion, the Marcos began the rule-setting process by setting simple, understandable, and attainable rules for their boys:

Rule 1. Do put your dirty clothes in the hamper.
Rule 2. Do leave a toy alone if someone else is holding it.
Rule 3. Do come when called.
Rule 4. Do chew with your mouth closed.
Rule 5. Do wait your turn.
Rule 6. Do get along with each other.

As they had decided, these rules governed not only chores, which the Marcos decided would be good for the boys to start doing, but they also put right before their noses the expectations that their parents had for getting along with family members in harmony. Once the rules were set, all Jill had to say was, "What's the rule about sharing?" or "What's the rule about chewing when you're eating?" When someone was participating in behavior that was "off the chart," having the boys quote the rule not only reinforced it but also helped make the rule a permanent investment in their memory banks.

Enforce rules. Setting rules is only the first step in developing self-discipline. Once rules are selected and presented to your children, letting them know what will happen when they follow the rules and what will befall them when they don't are the next building blocks in the plan to construct self-disciplined young people — and adults.

WARNING: AVOID CORPORAL PUNISHMENT.

Punishing children harshly for not following the rules only makes them angry and resentful. It also teaches them to avoid the adults who punish rather than making them want to follow the rules.

Teachable Moment

"Now that you know the rule about leaving a toy alone if someone else has it in his hand, let me tell you what will happen when you try to take it away," Jill explained to her sons after telling them about the new family rules. "The toy will go into time-out for the rest of the day, and you will go to time-out, too." (For a definition of time-out, please see page 50.)

"When you follow the rule," Jill said matter-of-factly, "you will be able to play with your toys and each other."

This consequence taught the Marco children to choose to play according to the rules in order to receive the benefits of doing so — a lesson that will serve them well throughout their lives.

Setting the rules gave the boys goals and expectations for their behavior, and telling them about the consequences helped them make decisions about their behavior before trouble started.

Praise children's behavior frequently when they follow rules. How will children ever know when something they've done is praiseworthy? You're in charge of that behavior — so be sure to praise your children's appropriate following of the rules by describing to them what they have done and why it was so admirable.

Teachable Moment

Whenever the Marcos saw a rule being followed, they would announce this good news with loads of verbal praise.

"Look at you, Bobby, you let your brother play with that toy until he put it down. You were following the sharing rule and that helped everyone have fun playing," Jill commented. "You remembered to put your dirty clothes in the hamper before you got in the bath, too. That was a big help to me; thanks for following the rule."

Later that day, Jill noticed that Carl would come into her room when she called his name, something he had been remiss in doing. To reinforce this giant step of behaving appropriately, Jill was delighted to provide a compliment. "Carl, you came right away when I called you. It's so nice of you to pay attention like that!"

Everyone at the Marcos household seemed happier because they were focusing on the positives, the right behavior of family members.

By praising their behavior with statements that described it specifically, Jill was able not only to remind the boys about the rules but also to illustrate the importance of following them, which increased the likelihood that these would be followed again.

Use lists and charts for older children. When helping older children become more self-disciplined, making lists and charts reminds them of what to do without your having to feel like the world's biggest nag. Lists provide an external structure that is neutral (as opposed to a human being, who can be seen as "the enemy"). This external reminder will soon become internalized, which is the goal of self-discipline, as the child follows the list each day.

Older children often resent being told what to do all the time, so following lists and charts allows them to get organized while clutching to their independence and gravitating toward self-discipline. Creating a simple "rule book" or posted sheet of rules is also helpful for older children, as well as for parents, so that rules can be looked up when family members forget how the rule is actually stated. The rule book reduces arguments and disagreements about just what had been mutually agreed upon, helping everyone stay on the same side of family goal-setting. When there is no "enemy camp," self-discipline is more likely to be reached.

Teachable Moment

When Tony's brother, Doug, came with his family to visit the Marcos, his children, aged seven, eleven, and thirteen, were often as out of control as Tony's children had been. After seeing what Jill and Tony had done with their little ones, Doug and his wife, Gina, decided to try some of the same rule-setting strategies. They made charts for chores that each child would do every day, and cleared their children's schedule so that they would have the time to complete them. In addition to the chore charts, they began a rule book in which they put the rules they were deciding that the family needed.

When explaining the rule book, Doug said, "You're all usually late for breakfast each morning, so we're going to have a new rule. In order to watch TV in the morning before school, you have to be at the breakfast table, dressed and ready for school, by seven-fifteen. I'll write that here in the rule book."

When they saw the children following the rules, they piled on the positive feedback in specific praise for doing so, which would help their children know they had made a good choice about their behavior. Rule violations would receive a natural consequence that would help their children make amends for their choice of behavior without feeling bad about themselves.

"I'm sorry you chose not to follow the rule," Gina said to one of the children. "Now you'll have to wait for the school bus in the other room without TV. Maybe tomorrow you'll get to watch with the rest of us while you wait for the bus."

The use of such natural consequences helped their children learn that their behavior choices create outcomes — and they are in control as to what those outcomes are, based on the choices they make. Again, rules act as guides, and the consequences encourage following the guides.

Help children set goals and follow them. When children want certain things, they can be masters at coercing their parents into buying them. In order to become self-disciplined, children must learn to set goals for themselves, to decide upon what steps will be needed to reach their goals, and to consistently work toward doing so. In this way, they avoid power struggles, manipulation tactics, and feelings of being out of the driver's seat in their own car of life.

WARNING: AVOID RESCUING CHILDREN FROM FAILURE.

When children set goals and then lose interest in achieving them, parents often want to rescue them from disappointment by getting them what they wanted anyway. Letting them reach the goal without working for it does not allow children to learn to cope with disappointment and teaches them an unhealthy lesson — that they can get what they want with little effort.

Teachable Moment

When five-year-old Carl wanted a new toy he saw on TV, his mom didn't open her wallet the next time they were at the mall.

"How much does it cost?" she asked matter-of-factly.

When he said that he didn't know, she said, "Next time we go to the mall, we'll look at the price."

After they had found out the price, Carl and his mom made a box with a picture of the toy on it and put it on his desk in his room. He could put his money in the box and count it from time to time to see how close he was getting to the goal.

When he wanted to spend his money on candy or gum, Jill would ask him whether or not he still had the toy in mind as the most favorite thing that he wanted in the whole wide world.

"I thought you were saving for a toy?" Jill queried. "Are you sure you want to spend your money for this candy now?"

Usually, Carl would reflect for a minute, put his money back in his pocket, and smile, knowing that he had made the choice all by himself to save his "spending" money!

Teach cooperation. Children who work for tangible rewards such as stickers, money, or a cookie, for example, learn only to expect to always be externally rewarded for their behavior. Rather than becoming self-disciplined, they become dependent on others to control their behavior by motivating them to make positive choices in order to reap the extra prize. Keep the motivation internal by pointing out how much it helped you to have your son carry in the family's groceries, for example, instead of his running from the car into the backyard to play when you both came home from the grocery store.

Teachable Moment

"Every time you put your dirty clothes in the hamper, I'll give you a sticker for your chart," Jill told her boys.

A few weeks later when she asked them to pick up their toys and put them away, one asked, "How many stickers will we get?" Rather than wanting to be cooperative, the boys were now deciding on whether or not to choose to do something based on how much they were rewarded for everything they did.

Jill decided to explain how much time she saved when the boys loaded up the hamper by themselves and thanked them with big hugs for the contribution to the family. By the proud looks in her sons' faces, they demonstrated that they had learned the important lesson of feeling good about helping someone — and were motivated to continue to be self-disciplined enough to do so, even if they would rather do something else than pick up their toys or dirty clothes.

Model self-discipline yourself. Even though it is difficult to do so, you can best teach your children self-discipline through the model you present. It is tempting to fly off the handle with anger sometimes when you are mad at something that happened at work or at home. But trying to self-talk your way to a calmer mood and problem-solve solutions rather than bang the pots and pans around the stove in disgust demonstrates your ability to practice what you teach. It is difficult to teach self-discipline if you have not learned it yourself.

Teachable Moment

Jill was hot! It had been one of those days at work. When she came home at 5:30, everything that could go wrong did. The oven was not working, she realized after twenty minutes, when she couldn't smell dinner cooking. She sat down at the kitchen table and wanted to cry.

Carl asked her what was wrong. She nearly screamed at him but instead mustered all the self-discipline she could, saying, "Mommy's had a hard day. I'm upset that dinner won't be ready now like I'd planned because the oven's broken. What should we do?" she asked quietly and sadly.

Much to her delight, her mood was met with empathy. "I'm sad, too," said Carl. "But I have some birthday money. I'll take the family out to dinner!"

Jill smiled for the first time that day. The two of them made a list of options for dinner, and after weighing the consequences of each, decided to take Carl up on his idea. It was a special night they talked about for years — truly a "lemonade made out of lemons"!

"It is good to have an end to journey toward; but it is the journey that matters, in the end." — URSULA K. LE GUIN

COOPERATION

"We cannot live only for ourselves. A thousand fibers connect us with our fellow men; and among those fibers, as sympathetic threads, our actions run as causes, and they come back to us as effects." — HERMAN MELVILLE

co·op·er·ate *vb.* **1.** to act or work with another or others; act together **2.** to associate with another or others for mutual benefit

○ "I'll get the groceries out of the car for you. I like to do my part."

○ "Let's work together on cleaning up the kitchen. That way it'll go faster."

○ "If we hurry, we can get this done so we can watch TV."

○ "I think it's fun for us all to work together like this."

THIS FINAL VIRTUE IN this book is, perhaps, a fitting summary of all nineteen other virtues. When a child behaves with honesty, respect, and empathy, for example, then he will naturally cooperate with others, because he respects them, can put himself in their shoes, and will treat them fairly. Cooperative children do not necessarily do everything a person tells them to do. In fact, looking out for others' welfare, as well as one's own, makes cooperation work. Particularly as our lives become busier, the less time we have to be unwilling to compromise and be selfish. By cooperating, everyone gets a chance to feel special and worthy — the ultimate goal of a democratic, cooperative society.

"J think cooperation is very important like if two people don't agree but have to be at a certain place at an exact time but have only one car." — JOYCE

WHAT DO WE MEAN BY COOPERATION?

- "None of us is as smart as all of us" is a positive motto that underlies cooperating.
- To cooperate, one must develop a sense of higher duty, an obligation to the higher good.
- Looking at work and play from another person's viewpoint helps a person know how to cooperate with him.
- When cooperating, one must be willing to combine forces to reach goals.
- Collaboration is an important ingredient in cooperation.

MEET THE KIM FAMILY

Philip and Patricia Kim wanted their nine-year-old son, Ronnie, and six-year-old son, Doug, to learn to cooperate with other children in school, but the boys were much more interested in pursuing their own selfish interests — including looking through soccer magazines and baseball cards instead of listening to others in their cooperative learning groups. Would they grow up to be more concerned about having a good time than about what was good for others? The Kims rarely did anything together as a family because

Ronnie simply didn't want to do what his parents had planned. Patricia was feeling overwhelmed with life as a parent and nagged Ronnie and Doug constantly about taking care of their dog, Prince, and their cat, Dolly, as well as their rooms. She knew that their feeling like a family was dependent on everyone cooperating to help run the household and sharing experiences, even those as simple as going to a baseball game or out to dinner together. With a goal of wanting to instill that virtue of cooperation in their children, Patricia and Philip started to evaluate their own behavior and how it reflected on these shining stars called children they loved so much.

TEACHING TOOLS

Encourage sharing. Living cooperatively within a family involves learning to share, and sharing requires a person to transcend his own self-interest and defer to the needs of others. To teach sharing, it is important to set some basic ground rules. With children in the preschool age group, the sharing rule would state that what a child has in his hand, he gets to keep. When he puts it down, it becomes free for others to use; if a toy causes trouble, it is put away for twenty-four hours. With older children, the abstract concept of sharing, as it involves cooperation with others, can be more easily understood. Rules for middle-years children and for teens involve reinforcing their thinking of the needs of others and what everyone will gain from an activity.

Teachable Moment

Six-year-old Doug came into the kitchen complaining that his older brother, Ronnie, wouldn't let him have a turn at playing the video game. Patricia immediately went to Ronnie and asked why he wouldn't share with his brother. (Later she realized that intervening in a sibling squabble was the wrong thing to do, because it only *increases* sibling rivalry.)

"Why can't Doug play with you?" Patricia asked. "You have another set of controls, so you can play together."

"I don't want to play with him because he isn't any good," came the blunt answer.

"Then if you won't play with him, you'll have to figure out a way he can share the game with you," Patricia mandated. "I'll give you ten minutes to come up with a plan for sharing the game. When you figure out a plan, you'll get to play some more. Otherwise, I'll turn it off."

"I know what we'll do," came Ronnie's quick reply. He knew his mother meant business and would take the game away. "We'll take turns. I'll get the timer from the kitchen, and we'll each have, ummm, let's say fifteen minutes."

"Ronnie, what an excellent idea!" Patricia praised. "But who'll go first?"

"We could flip for it," chimed in little Doug, who had just learned how to do heads-or-tails.

After the boys worked out a sharing rule, Patricia noticed that the kitchen timer was next to the video game more than it was in the kitchen. She didn't mind, though, because the boys were sharing the game. She often praised them for their maturity in figuring out a solution to the sharing problem and for sticking to the plan.

"Isn't it nice that both of you get to play?" she commented as she watched Ronnie coaching his little brother as he maneuvered through a particularly difficult part of a game. "And, Ronnie, you're helping Doug play, too."

"Yeah, and he's really getting good," came Ronnie's excited reply. "He can almost beat me now. We play together lots now."

Patricia was pleased with their sharing and cooperation. She also realized that she would have to encourage the same problem-solving and sharing in other areas, such as deciding who sat in the coveted front seat in the car, so that cooperation would become a "game" they played in other aspects of their lives, too.

"Cooperate and compromise are like the sun and moon. They both give off good light." — RACHEL

Encourage playing the game. Today's children seem to enjoy sports more than ever before, but often they lose sight of the fun of playing because of the highly competitive atmosphere of so many organized games and the over-zealous parents who encourage the notion that "winning is everything." Team sports can encourage working together in cooperation in order for all to benefit. But when parents, coaches, and children focus on a "win at all costs" attitude, they lose sight of the more cooperative and shared joy of "let's have fun" playing. The advantage of a focus on playing versus winning is that it moves children away from intense self-centered competitiveness to an awareness of sharing and cooperation, thereby allowing everyone to have more fun.

To teach children cooperation and sharing in team sports, emphasize the joy of playing together and improving skills rather than focusing on the outcome of the game. Praising effort, cooperation, and team spirit while moving children's focus away from the win/lose decision of competition will decrease the stress children experience in intense competition and will help them understand the value of the process of play — the fun of trying one's best and being proud of that effort.

Teachable Moment

"I hate them!" Ronnie exclaimed loudly after a soccer game. "They beat us last time, too."

"But I thought most of those boys were your friends," Philip said.

"But, Dad, they always win," Ronnie whined.

"Is winning so important that you'd hate your friends because they won a couple of games?" Philip continued. "Maybe you shouldn't play soccer, because you get so upset."

"But I want to win!" Ronnie shouted. "We're just a bunch of losers."

"How does losing a game make you a loser?" Philip was determined to try to get Ronnie to see the fallacy in his reasoning.

"Dad, you have to win to be a winner!" he said impatiently.

"I thought it was fun just to play. When did winning get to be so important?"

"Doesn't everybody want to win?" Ronnie asked, now puzzled at his dad's reasoning.

"It seems to me that winning is nice, but just getting to play with your friends and getting better at what you're doing should be the most important parts of the game," Philip reasoned.

"But our coach wants us to win," Ronnie argued. "What if we just went out and messed around and lost all the time?"

"Well, I think you should try your hardest and play your best each time. That way you know you did your best.

Even if the score doesn't say you won, you at least played a good game. Understand?"

"I guess," Ronnie answered. "If I play hard and always do my best, we might win."

"Look at the way you set up that goal kick in the first half!" Philip reminded him. "You gave a really great effort, and you were all really excited. It must have felt good to work as a team and to play so well together."

Philip was satisfied that his son was at least thinking about the process of play rather than the end result. He knew the overemphasis on winning wasn't healthy and was determined to try to keep him focused on building his skills and on teamwork, instead of only the final score.

Encourage healthy competition. Competition is a good motivator as long as it isn't a goal in itself. One arena that encourages unhealthy competition is school itself — a hotbed of "better grades" battles, wars over test results, and stressful skill evaluations ad nauseam. The move toward creating more cooperative learning groups in which children are encouraged to work together on projects so that they learn not only necessary academic skills but also how to problem-solve and negotiate with other students has begun to return to classrooms. Children who learn to work in cooperation with each other develop an understanding of meeting the needs of the group, rather than remaining wholly self-centered and self-absorbed, interested only in making themselves successful.

Teachable Moment

"Mom, look at the social studies project on Japan I brought home today," Ronnie announced excitedly.

"Wow! This is a great-looking project," Patricia said as

she turned the pages of the big spiral notebook. "What grade did you get?"

"We didn't get a grade," Ronnie answered. "It was a cooperative learning project that our team worked on together."

"But how do you know how well you did if there isn't a grade?" Patricia pursued.

"We got feedback sheets that told us what the strengths of the project were and then told us what we could do to make it better," Ronnie answered patiently.

"Were the feedback sheets graded?" Patricia continued. "How will you know whether you did well or not?"

"That's not important, Mom," Ronnie answered. "We had fun working together on the project, and we all learned a lot about Japan."

"Did everyone work on the project, or did some of the team goof off and let other kids do most of the work?" Patricia asked.

"We aren't allowed to hitchhike," Ronnie answered. "We took the topic we chose, broke it down into what needed to be done, and each one of us got a part to do. That way nobody got out of doing the work. We had to wait for Sara's part, because she was sick for a couple of days. She worked on it at home, though. We took all the parts and put it together into this big folder. Then each team presented the project to the class. Jennie gets to take the folder home tomorrow to show her mom."

Patricia began to realize the value of what her son was learning. It was obvious from the size of the folder with his Japan project in it that considerable effort must have taken place in this class over the past several weeks. Not only that, but Ronnie seemed to understand the value of working together to get something done. He was learning more than facts about a country — he was learning to cooperate and to be a part of a team.

Set family goals. When family goals are set and everyone is encouraged to work toward meeting them, family members learn to cooperate with each other in order to reach a common finish line. To help your family learn cooperation, begin by establishing short-term, easily attainable goals that everyone is interested in reaching. A weekly dinner out, renting or going to a movie, having a favorite dish, and watching a favorite TV program together are but a few simple goals that all may be willing to cooperate to achieve. Once the goal is set, then the steps needed to reach the goal must be established. Getting along with each other for the week, keeping rooms clean, putting the dinner dishes in the sink, making their beds every day, and doing other chores could be the building blocks needed to be put in place in order to reach a previously agreed-upon end result.

WARNING: BE SURE THAT THE GOAL IS ATTAINABLE AND THAT YOUR CHILDREN CAN BE SUCCESSFUL IN REACHING THE GOAL THE FIRST TIME.

After meeting with initial success, your family can make the goals harder to reach and the standards for reaching them higher.

Teachable Moment

At dinner, Philip announced, "We need to do more as a family. Working together to get something we all want is one way your mom and I decided we could do that. What do you think?"

"What do you mean, work together?" Ronnie asked cautiously.

"Well, there are lots of things that a family needs to have done so that it can be a good family. What I would like for you to do every day is to make your beds and put your dirty clothes in the clothes hamper in the bathroom. That's all."

"I don't see why I have to make my bed," Ronnie said scornfully. "I just mess it up again when I get in it. What's the point?"

"The point is that a made bed makes your room look more tidy and teaches you to be neat. That's important for a family, because if we didn't keep things neat, pretty soon everything would be so messy that we couldn't even get into the house."

"Tell you what let's do," Patricia joined in. "I know you can try to remember each day to make your bed and put your dirty clothes in the hamper. If you do that for the week, then next Friday we'll all go to the video store and rent something we all would like to watch."

Philip handed Ronnie a piece of paper with boxes on it for each day of the week and the words "Make bed" and "Clothes in hamper" on it.

"Here are some checklists so you can remember to do these two things every day. That way, when you cooperate, we all get to do something fun," Philip continued, pleased that everyone would benefit from the team effort the family was committed to making.

Create a sense of collaboration. Children who learn how to collaborate learn how to include "give and take" in their repertoire, to make life's little climbs uphill become less tiring. Teach your children how collaborating helps everyone benefit and, perhaps, be happier than if one person had gone to the finish line alone.

Teachable Moment

"You dweeb. You are so stupid," Ronnie said to his little brother, Doug. "I want to get this fort built and all you're doing is getting in the way. Now get out of here!"

"All right for you," came Doug's reply. "I don't care if you ever get this done. You probably won't let me play in it anyway." And off Doug went into the house.

In overhearing this put-down, Patricia decided that her children not only needed to learn how to get along better with each other but also needed to reduce the "war" between the brothers and increase their desire to collaborate. She decided that a little encouragement might help the cause of peace and cooperation.

"Ronnie, how could you get your fort built more quickly and easily?" she asked.

"I need some help," he replied. "Will you help me?"

"I'm sorry I can't help," she answered. "I have lots of things to do in the house, and they'll take all day. Who else could you get to help?"

"Dad could help, but he's not home," Ronnie whined.

"How about your brother?" she asked innocently. "Maybe he could help."

"No, he's too little, and he doesn't know how to do anything. He only gets in the way."

"Well, maybe if you two worked together, you'd get finished sooner and would be able to play in the fort. Think about it! If you need help, he's here," she said as she went back into the house.

Later that day, she observed Ronnie and Doug working

together to solve the fort problem. Ronnie had enlisted the help of his little brother with the promise that if they worked together, Doug would also get to play in the fort.

"Come on, Doug, you hold that end and I'll hold this one, and we can get this board up on top," Ronnie told his little brother. "If we work hard on it, I think we can finish it today. Then we can play in it."

She watched from the window as the boys worked together and the crude fort made of old boxes and scraps of wood took shape. Later, she noticed how much fun they were having playing together in their handiwork.

"You boys really did well building your fort," Patricia told them when they came in for a snack. "You must really feel proud of what you were able to do together."

"Yeah," Doug volunteered. "Ron was having a hard time, but we both did it together, and now we can play in it as much as we want."

"And next, we're going to get some more old lumber and stuff and start a tree house in the mulberry tree," Ronnie said enthusiastically.

"See how much fun it is to join forces to get things done," Patricia commented, and the boys happily agreed before going off again to play in their masterpiece.

Patricia was pleased that her little push had gotten the ball rolling toward teaching her boys to collaborate. With a little maintenance, this trend should continue as Doug and Ronnie began to appreciate the true rewards in joining forces to get things done.

Praise cooperation. Praising children when they cooperate increases the chance that they'll find cooperation a pleasant experience that they'll want to repeat. To help your children increase their desire to get along with each other in give-and-take fashion, at home and with others on the playground and in class, describe their behavior (and that of your spouse and others) to them when they are cooperating.

WARNING: AVOID GETTING ANGRY AND PUNISHING YOUR CHILDREN WHEN THEY CHOOSE NOT TO COOPERATE.

Punishment won't increase a child's desire to cooperate with a parent who inflicts pain.

Teachable Moment

Philip came home from a few hours of extra work at the office one Saturday to find Ronnie hard at work cleaning the house. "Wow!" he exclaimed. "You are really working hard. Thank you for being so cooperative. I'm going to take you to the park this afternoon for working so hard."

"Thanks for helping me clean up after dinner," Patricia said that evening as she witnessed the unthinkable: Ronnie was helping clear the table without her nagging him to do so.

"It was my job today," Ronnie answered.

"I know, dear. But I just had to tell you how nice it is to have your help. Now we're finished and we can go for a walk before it gets dark. Thanks again for cooperating."

The next day, Patricia found Doug busily making his bed. "You're working so hard to make your bed look nice. I really appreciate your help." Somehow, keeping their home neater became more meaningful to the boys when they knew their parents were noticing and appreciating their efforts.

Reinforce children's connection to the family. Children who are told they are important in a family have a greater sense of self-esteem because they "belong" to a group who considers them valuable. To help your children gain a sense of being needed, take every opportunity to point out their importance to the family unit. Thanking them frequently for their help and positive attitude increases their sense of being valuable to the people whose opinion they most respect.

Teachable Moment

"I don't know how our family would survive without your help," Patricia told Ronnie as he helped her clean the house.

"Yeah, it's kind of fun to work together like this," her son beamed with pleasure.

"It feels good to be a part of this family," Patricia admitted, even though she didn't like all the work she had to do either.

Life wasn't always a bed of roses, Patricia had learned even as a child, but focusing on the positives — the beautiful flowers — gave her more pleasure than only thinking of the negatives — the prickly, ugly thorns.

"Your sole contribution to the sum of things is yourself." — FRANK CRANE

POSTSCRIPT

You know that you are responsible for teaching your children to eat with a fork, to tie their shoes, to use the toilet, and even for encouraging them to read and write. But the education of children is not complete without the lessons of character and virtue that fill this book, lessons that help them learn how to have the most fulfilling and meaningful experience humans can have — caring about themselves, their friends, their family, their community.

Through exercises, experience, and example — most of all, example — you can be sure that the lessons in this book that you most want your children to learn will be passed on to them . . . for how else will they be transmitted to the next generation if we do not meaningfully and purposefully apply ourselves to doing so? When individuals consciously and committedly use their energy to teach kindness, respect, and compassion, we have seen the remarkable results — both the student and teacher of these virtues feels happier, more satisfied, and renewed.

Where have we witnessed the powerful effects of teaching these virtues? We have had this amazing experience happen right before our very eyes as we have seen schools all across the country reap the benefits of incorporating the award-winning school-based educational program called "Kindness Is Contagious . . . Catch It!" into their curriculums. Each school's student and administrative population reports that discipline and academic performances improved dramatically, as did the overall climate for learning, when everyone believed in the common goal of caring about each other.

We are confident that the universally agreed-upon components of fine character and virtue in this book are best taught through the combined modeling and mentoring of the two most influential sources of children's learning—parents and formally trained educators, who have always worked together to strengthen the knowledge of the younger generation.

We hope that you are encouraged and energized by the lessons of virtue your family is experiencing as you use this book's "Teachable Moments" in your everyday interactions. As you create your own special ways to pass on lessons of virtue, we hope you share how they have helped strengthen the caring relationships in your family, so that other families can benefit from your experiences. If you would like to share them with us, please do so by sending them to Teachable Virtues, P.O. Box 12045, Overland Park, KS 66212.

"Never doubt that a small group of thoughtful, committed citizens can change the world. Indeed it is the only thing that ever has." —MARGARET MEAD